ROUTLEDGE LIBRARY EDITIONS:
HISTORY OF EDUCATION

THE CHANGING
CURRICULUM

# THE CHANGING CURRICULUM

*By*

HISTORY OF EDUCATION SOCIETY

Volume 10

LONDON AND NEW YORK

First published in 1971

This edition first published in 2007 by
Routledge
2 Park Square, Milton Park, Abingdon, Oxon OX14 4RN

Simultaneously published in the USA and Canada
by Routledge
711 Third Avenue, New York, NY 10017

Transferred to Digital Printing 2007

*Routledge is an imprint of the Taylor & Francis Group, an informa business*

First issued in paperback 2013

© 1971 History of Education Society

All rights reserved. No part of this book may be reprinted or reproduced or utilised in any form or by any electronic, mechanical, or other means, now known or hereafter invented, including photocopying and recording, or in any information storage or retrieval system, without permission in writing from the publishers.

*British Library Cataloguing in Publication Data*
A catalogue record for this book is available from the British Library

*Library of Congress Cataloging in Publication Data*
A catalog record for this book has been requested

ISBN13: 978-0-415-43238-2 (hardback)
ISBN13: 978-0-415-86057-4 (paperback)
ISBN13: 978-0-415-41978-9 (set)

**Publisher's Note**
The publisher has gone to great lengths to ensure the quality of this reprint but points out that some imperfections in the original copies may be apparent.

HISTORY OF
EDUCATION SOCIETY

# The changing curriculum

*Published by*
METHUEN & CO LTD
*11 New Fetter Lane London EC4*

*First published 1971*
*by Methuen & Co Ltd*
*11 New Fetter Lane, London EC4*
*© 1971 by History of Education Society*
*Set in Press Roman by*
*E.W.C. Wilkins & Associates, Ltd*
*London*
*Printed in Great Britain by*
*Redwood Press,*
*Trowbridge, Wilts.*
*SBN 416 08690 X*

Distributed in the U.S.A.
by Barnes & Noble Inc.

# Contents

| | |
|---|---|
| HISTORY OF EDUCATION SOCIETY | viii |
| PREFACE | x |
| INTRODUCTION | xi |
| **R.R. BOLGAR** Humanist education and its contribution to the Renaissance | 1 |
| **CHARLES WEBSTER** Science and the challenge to the scholastic curriculum 1640–1660 | 21 |
| **W.H.G. ARMYTAGE** Augustan academic honeycombs: some eighteenth-century conventicles of science | 37 |
| **H.C. MORGAN** The curriculum of training in the fine arts in the nineteenth century | 51 |
| **W.H. BROCK** Prologue to heurism | 71 |
| **E.G. EDWARDS** The need for a history of higher education | 87 |
| INDEX | 101 |

# History of education society

| | |
|---|---|
| Chairman | David Bradshaw (Principal, Doncaster College of Education) |
| Vice-Chairman | Professor Brian Simon (Leicester University School of Education) |
| Secretary | Ian Taylor (St John's College, York) |
| Treasurer | Trevor Hearl (St Paul's College, Cheltenham) |
| Editor of the Bulletin | T.G. Cook (Cambridge University Department of Education) |
| Other Committee Members | Professor W.H.G. Armytage (Sheffield University Department of Education) |
| | Professor Kenneth Charlton (Birmingham University School of Education) |
| | Malcolm Seaborne (Leicester University School of Education) |
| | Nanette Whitbread (City of Leicester College of Education) |

The aim of the Society, founded in 1967, is to further the study of the History of Education by providing opportunities for discussion among those engaged in its study and teaching.

Conferences. and meetings are organized, a Bulletin is published twice a year in Spring and Autumn and other publications pertaining to the History of Education are sponsored.

Membership is open to all connected in a professional capacity with education, or engaged in the study or teaching of the History of

Education. Overseas members are welcomed and are offered a specially reduced subscription rate. Libraries are invited to subscribe to the Bulletin only; otherwise Society membership is individual not institutional.

| *Annual Subscriptions* | Members | £2 |
| | Overseas Members (surface mail) | £1 |
| | Student Members | 50p |
| | Libraries | £1 |
| *Life Membership* | | £25 |

# Preface

The success of the volume of conference papers issued last year under the title of *Studies in the Government and Control of Education since 1860* has encouraged the History of Education Society to arrange for the publication of the papers given at its conference held at Coventry College of Education in December 1969. The theme of the conference was 'The Changing Curriculum' and all the main papers given are included in this volume, together with a contribution by Dr R.R. Bolgar of King's College, Cambridge, whose lecture given at our London conference at Easter 1970 appeared to us to form an admirable starting-point for the rest of the book.

The Society is grateful to Messrs Methuen and Co for again undertaking the publication of our papers, and to Mr Malcolm Seaborne for preparing them for publication. We are also indebted to Mr T.G. Cook who saw the book through the press and to Mr D.S. Hempsall who compiled the index.

Enquiries about membership of the Society, which is open to all engaged in teaching or studying the subject, should be addressed to the Secretary, Mr Ian Taylor, at St John's College, York, Y03 7EX.

David C.A. Bradshaw
Principal, Doncaster College of Education
*Chairman, History of Education Society*

# Introduction

There has in recent years been a renewed interest in the whole field of curriculum development, but relatively little account has so far been taken of the historical aspects of curriculum change. The constant revision of what is taught in schools and universities has always been essential for progress in educational thought and practice. Sometimes it is the force of some well-defined external circumstance — such as that commonly attributed to the launching of Sputnik I in relation to scientific and technical education — which appears to stimulate change. But often the reasons why new movements gain momentum are more complex and the skills of the historian are therefore more necessary than ever in helping to elucidate them.

The first of the papers printed in this volume, by Dr R.R. Bolgar of King's College, Cambridge, considers the relationship between the achievements of the Renaissance and the education provided during this crucial period of change. He shows that in origin the Renaissance appeared to owe little directly to the educational system of its day and that by the time the humanists had come in their turn to influence the school curriculum, their creative drive was nearly spent. It was against the formalism of the accepted curriculum of the late sixteenth and early seventeenth centuries that the innovators of the Civil War period reacted. The contribution made by the educationists of this period, who drew their inspiration from science rather than the classics, is discussed by Mr Charles Webster of Corpus Christi College, Oxford, in his paper on 'Science and the challenge to the scholastic curriculum 1640–1660'. Rarely has so short a period of educational history produced so many fruitful ideas; yet Mr Webster shows that this new creative movement in turn spent itself and made relatively little change in the official educational system.

After 1660, new developments tended to find expression in unofficial and informal ways. So far as the vital growth of science and technology was concerned, Professor W.H.G. Armytage of Sheffield University gives a fascinating glimpse — indeed, a veritable kaleidoscope of colourful detail — in his paper describing how men interested in scientific and technological change formed themselves into groups of various kinds in all parts of Europe — what he calls the 'academic honeycombs' of the eighteenth century.

Coming to the nineteenth century, Dr H.C. Morgan of St John's

College, York, deals with the development of art education, both 'private' in the shape of the Royal Academy and 'public' in the shape of the Science and Art Department. Again his paper illustrates the strength of tradition, in this case deriving from the ideas first elaborated in England by Sir Joshua Reynolds. Dr W.H. Brock of Leicester University follows with a discussion of the work of scientific innovators of the Victorian period and how it was that Henry Armstrong managed to break into the accepted system of scientific training with the concept of heuristic teaching.

Finally, Dr E.G. Edwards, Vice-Chancellor of Bradford University, discusses 'The need for a history of higher education'. His paper helps to put the present expansion of higher education into perspective and he makes the point which the other papers in this collection seem to exemplify, that the study of the history of education should not lead to an uncritical respect for tradition; rather, as Dr Edwards remarks, it 'prepares us for surprise in the nature of the movement of society' in the present as well as the past.

Malcolm Seaborne<br>University of Leicester

R. R. BOLGAR

# Humanist education and its contribution to the Renaissance

The word 'humanist' made its appearance during the fifteenth century when its Latin form *'humanista'* was used to denote a teacher of grammar. Later its meaning widened, until it came by imperceptible degrees to cover all serious students of ancient Greek and Latin [1]. But, later still, there was yet another change. About a hundred years ago, 'humanist', without quite losing its traditional sense of 'classical scholar', was gradually restricted to the classical scholars of the Renaissance. It became customary to refer to Petrarch as a humanist, but to deny the name to Dante who was thought to belong to the Middle Ages. Lambinus, Thomas Smith, Buchanan and Dorat, all of whom died between 1570 and 1590, figured as humanists, but historians hesitated to apply the term to a Casaubon or a Savile who lived only a generation later.

For the modern reader humanism is the classical learning of the Renaissance, and the epoch during which it flourished covers three centuries from 1300 to 1600. They were centuries of prodigious change when the modern world was born. The humanist age witnessed the first flowering of the vernaculars and saw them produce literatures that offered to match the achievements of Greece and Rome. It saw the birth of modern science, the invention of algebra, the shattering of the Ptolemaic universe, critical advances in optics, metallurgy, zoology and systematic botany. It saw the transformation of historiography, the Machiavellian separation of politics from ethics. New styles evolved in architecture. Painting from Giotto to Titian produced masterpieces far superior to anything the world had seen before. And side by side with these developments came profound social changes. The religious life of Europe took on a more practical and more personal form, while the power of feudal aristocracy began to pass with revolutionary effects to a rich middle class of merchants and newly established landowners.

These impressive changes all seem to have had links of some sort with the study of antiquity which the humanists fostered. Vernacular literature drew upon ancient themes and revived ancient genres. Science in many fields, including some branches of mathematics, advanced from the points reached in ancient times. The debt of the architects to Vitruvius, the use made by painters of ancient mythology leap to the eye; and the religious movements of the period were plainly affected by the fashion for reading classical authors in the original which led to the idea of making a direct appeal to the Bible and to efforts to produce a more correct biblical text. The humanists themselves emphasized the importance of these links and were inclined to present all that was novel and interesting in the culture of their day as the product of classical learning. For Erasmus, for Rabelais, for the Pléiade, the progress which marked their age was nothing more or less than the recovery of the past.

Extreme claims always produce a reaction. Actually the humanists were lucky. The point of view they put forward met with general acceptance and held the field for centuries. We continued to take them at their own valuation right up to the time of Burckhardt's *Civilisation of the Renaissance*. However, eventually, in our own day the reaction did materialize.

> The more we look into the question, the harder we shall find it to believe that humanism had any power of encouraging, or any wish to encourage, the literature that actually arose ... [2]

> All the facts seem consistent with the view that the great literature of the fifteen-eighties and nineties was something which humanism, with its unities and *Gorboducs* and English hexameters, would have prevented if it could ... [3]

> In the field of philosophy humanism must be regarded quite frankly as a Philistine movement: even an obscurantist movement . . . [4]

These rather tart comments are taken from the obvious source for such criticisms: C.S.Lewis's well-known introduction to his *English Literature in the Sixteenth Century*. Lewis was not a pioneer in making this attack on humanism. He was voicing opinions which had been current among medievalists and students of Renaissance English for over a generation. Humanism has been in academic disgrace for a long time now — in this country, even if not in America or on the continent: which is perhaps the reason why we still lack in British universities lectureships specifically for the study of humanist Latin.

Our assessment of what the humanists achieved in education must depend to some degree on what we think they achieved in a general way. It is disturbing, therefore, to be faced with sharply divergent judgements. The humanists created the Renaissance. The humanists hindered the Renaissance. The truth may be reasonably supposed to lie somewhere between these vehement extremes. But its precise character does not promise to be easy to determine.

And this difficulty is not the only one we have to overcome. For when we turn to our own laborious speciality — the educational scene — we find ourselves once again poised between paradoxically divergent extremes. We face what appears to be a more than usually wide disparity between intention and achievement, between what we read in the writings of educational theorists, and what seems to have actually happened in the classroom.

The humanist writers on education put forward some wholly admirable aims. Studying ancient Greek and Latin was to produce men of affairs with sound judgement, eloquent orators and writers, courtiers whose intellectual, social and physical development attained a perfect harmony, encyclopedic scholars versed in every art and science. They saw themselves as the midwives of the universally competent man.

Read Vergerio's *De Ingenuis Moribus* [5] or even Ascham's *Scholemaster* [6], then turn to the *Consuetudinarium Scholae Etonensis* [7], and you are in for a surprise. The *Consuetudinarium* gives us an account of the timetable and curriculum at Eton in 1560. What we find seems at first sight very far from the high hopes of the theorists.

The document is a long one. So I shall confine myself to the doings of the top class. If there was to be education of a broad sort that is where we should expect to find it.

7 a.m. The monitor heard his classmates repeat by heart the Latin passage they had studied the previous day.

8 a.m. The master set a sentence which the boys then put into Latin verse.

9 a.m. The monitor recited to the master the previous day's passage. The boys were given a title on which to write a prose or verse theme. The master then read and explained, on Mondays and Tuesdays, a passage from a prose writer (Caesar or Cicero's *De Officiis* or *De Amicitia*), on Wednesdays and Thursdays, a passage from Virgil. From these readings the boys were to collect flowers of rhetoric: i.e. antitheses, epithets, synonyms, proverbs, similes, comparisons, anecdotes, descriptions of circumstances, places and people, fables, witticisms, figures of speech and apophthegms.

After this burst of activity they had a two-hour break for a meal. Then from midday they worked by themselves on their themes for an hour.

1 – 3 p.m. The master tested the boys giving them English sentences to translate which related to the passage he had read earlier.

3 p.m. The boys were set some Greek grammar to learn.

4 p.m. They were tested on this by the master, and their themes were marked.

5 – 6 p.m. They had supper and after supper they were tested by the monitor on the day's lessons.

To get this into perspective, we must be careful to notice that although the boys worked nine hours, the master taught only four: 9–10 p.m., 1–3 p.m., 4–5 p.m.; and during these times, he was dealing also with two other classes whose activities I have not mentioned. No class could therefore count on more than eighty minutes' teaching a day. The passage for the day was one of three which the master expounded during the last period of the morning after he had heard the monitors' lessons. It is evident that the exposition destined for a particular class could not have lasted much more than fifteen minutes. How many lines of Virgil can one translate and explain in a quarter of an hour? Ten would appear to be a very generous estimate [8].

All this seems on the face of it uninspiring and slapdash. A successful novelist describing his schooldays in the *New Statesman* could hardly evoke a worse picture of neglect, discomfort and boredom. Eton in the 1560s plainly carried out the precept traditionally attributed to an old Scottish dominie: 'It doesn't matter what you teach the little devils provided you make them hate it.' We find ourselves at the opposite pole from the high hopes the humanists cherished about their educational schemes. The hopes were too high; but is not the reality that seems to present itself in documents like the Eton *Consuetudinarium* too ugly to have been true?

I have not done more so far than just outline our problems. They are in a sense worse, more intransigent, than I have been able to suggest. The points of view I have indicated are not mere exaggerations. Take the cultural problem first. There is hard evidence to support both the theory that humanism contributed substantially to the Renaissance and the theory that it hampered rather than forwarded progress. This evidence must be accommodated, so that our task is not so much to find a mean as to achieve some sort of synthesis. Hegel, not Aristotle, must be our guide. And the same holds for the subsidiary, more precisely educational, issue. It is plain enough that the humanists were

## HUMANIST EDUCATION AND THE RENAISSANCE

not just talking nonsense like some dishonest school prospectus. The education they planned was not without its value, and the schools in which their plans were realized, the schools we read about in Sturm's *De Ludis Litterarum* [9], in the Eton *Consuetudinarium* and later in Brinsley and Hoole, turned out after all some eminent generations for all the dreariness of their programmes. Here again, what we have to do is to synthesize, to bring together contradictory impressions.

I do not propose to produce the necessary syntheses. All I have to offer are some suggestions as to the reasons for these puzzling polarities. Knowing *why* a difficulty has arisen often gives some lead to its solution. Problems, especially in history, are often created by the selection one has made among the facts, a selection which is often due to accidental circumstances. The data we have to hand when studying a period of history will depend
(a) on what has survived and
(b) on what the concerns of our predecessors led them to collect.
Where the volume of material which has survived is quite substantial, it is the second of these two factors, namely the interest pursued by earlier scholars, which tends to exert a decisive influence. And that is the case here. What we know about humanism has been shaped by the particular purposes for which scholars of earlier generations studied the achievements of the humanists. The view we obtain is therefore oddly restricted and in some ways misleading.

Put in these general terms the matter sounds unduly mysterious. What I have in mind is actually something quite simple. For obvious reasons the study of humanism cannot be separated from the study of the survival of the Greek and Roman classics; and this is particularly true when we consider, as C.S.Lewis did, the literary influence of the humanists. But, tracing the survival of classical authors — what Aby Warburg called *das Nachleben der Antike* — is a branch of study of comparatively recent growth. It made its appearance at the end of the last century, and its chief promoters were the great textual critics. When classical scholars in the 1830s came round to the idea of constructing genealogical tables of codices, the history of individual manuscripts — where they were copied, when, from what earlier version — became a matter of importance for textual scholarship, and it was an importance which the gradual acceptance of the principle *recentiores non deteriores* later in the century was to emphasize still further. By the time Wilamowitz came on the scene, men had realized that if a comparatively recent manuscript, copied perhaps round 1400 or 1500, could be shown by the construction of a chain of historical evidence to derive its readings from an early and perhaps lost tradition, a great step forward would be made in our knowledge of an author's text. A feat of this magnitude was not (I think) carried out successfully until Giuseppe Billanovich, just after the last war, identified the Harleian Livy, once in the possession of Petrarch, as recording in its marginal notes a tradition independent of our usual source for the text [10]. But the collection of materials on which such arguments could be built had been going on hopefully for decades before Billanovich turned them to such brilliant use. Data on who owned, cited, copied or edited the main classical authors make up a large part of Sandys's three-volume *History of Classical Scholarship*, published originally in the first decade of this century [11], and make up pretty well all that Manitius's great history of medieval Latin literature [12], completed in the 1930s, has to say about the influence exercised by classical authors. The fortunes of ancient literature in the Middle Ages and the Renaissance were studied in a way which was of great potential value for textual critics, but was not of much value to anyone else and was certainly not well chosen to give a picture of the impact which that literature made on the emergent vernaculars.

These techniques of investigation inspired by the needs of textual criticism form one side of the picture we want to consider. But the work of the humanists as a field of enquiry has, in another direction, close connections with the study of the new-born vernacular literatures. Poised between the ancient world and the modern, it was also affected by techniques which developed in the modern field.

The technique evolved by scholars in the modern field which came to affect humanist studies most decisively was the one the Germans call *Quellenforschung*, the tracing of borrowed material. As we all know, the first writers to use the vernaculars leant heavily on Latin models, often to the extent of translating whole passages. They imitated plots, characters, items of description, arguments, figures of speech, everything you can think of; and somewhere around 1890 locating such borrowed items became a major academic industry. This happened most blatantly in France where tomes were compiled on the borrowings of Rabelais, the Pléiade poets and Montaigne; but Shakespeare in England and Dante in Italy also came in for a good deal of attention. It was an impressively laborious but not a very fruitful form of scholarship. Genius may be an infinite capacity for taking pains but an infinite capacity for taking pains does not automatically produce a work of genius.

I remember some years back having to study Paul Laumonier's edition of Ronsard. Every three or four lines there was a note adducing a parallel from Pindar or Ovid. But Laumonier made no attempt to distinguish between actual translations, the borrowing of incidents or stories and the vaguest of vague echoes. Everything was grist to his mill, and all on the same level. The stuff he turned out has its value as a starting-point for somebody else's work. But in itself it is unspeakably dreary. It has little attraction for the literary critic or cultural historian, whose interest is in the results of borrowing and not the borrowing itself. Serious enquiry in this field ought to concentrate on what a later writer managed to make of his borrowed material. And that is an issue which the *Quellenforscher* of the 1930s and 1940s preferred to avoid. Reading them one gets the impression that our debt to antiquity had the character of a collection of bric-à-brac, an impression which is very far from the truth.

The polarity we have been examining — the awkward polarity between the views of Burckhardt and those of C.S.Lewis — can be seen therefore to have had its origin in the evidence they respectively used. It is not surprising that Burckhardt should have had a high opinion of humanist achievements since he based his assessment on humanist writings; and it is not surprising that Lewis should have underestimated these same achievements since he saw them in the light of the specialized research of the years immediately preceding 1954, a research which had been curiously restricted in its scope. A little learning is a dangerous thing; but great learning can be dangerous too if its objectives are narrow.

From all this it is possible to derive some comfort. Difficulties which spring from the character of one's evidence can disappear or become less obvious as that evidence is supplemented. Sixteen years have passed since Lewis published his *History*; and they have been years of exciting progress. The emphasis is shifting at last from the study of piecemeal borrowing to what might fairly be called the study of influences. Rhetoric in particular is receiving a good deal of attention. Some very interesting work has been done recently, for example, by B. Vickers on Bacon's style, and we may perhaps soon have a fairly clear picture of how humanist teachings and models affected stylistic developments in English and French. Another fruitful line has been the pursuit of various myths and classical stories through their different incarnations. Dido, to take one instance, figures first as a victim whose fall does not call for any moral judgement (the assumption being that any foreign queen is fair game for a visiting knight); then as a sinner doomed to Hell for illicit love; then in Boccaccio as a model of chastity (using the story in Justin where she dies to avoid remarriage); then as a heroine whose love was betrayed (this theme is introduced typically by the feminist Christine de Pisan); then as a victim of a malign fate. Finally in Marlowe we see her as a *maîtresse-femme*, addicted to having her own way and dying when frustrated. These versions became popular in successive generations and can in each case be related to the general outlook of the time. From studies of this type [13] we obtain what one can call a dynamic view of classical influences. We have an ancient legend acting as stimulus to produce a multitude of strange new developments.

And it is not just a question of legends. Similarly dynamic effects can be traced in the history of science. One has only to look at the kind of influence Diophantus exercised in mathematics or Dioscorides in botany.

It seems obvious that if research continues for another two decades along the paths which are being opened up, we shall come a long way towards showing that the classical heritage did play a decisive part in bringing about the Renaissance; and such a conclusion will lend considerable importance to the humanists in their turn.

We can accept this, and it is interesting. But its main effect is to bring us as educational historians up against another difficulty. We bridge one crevasse only to find ourselves in front of another. Assuming that the work of the humanists proved fruitful in its entirety, what connection had this work with the educational system that the humanists evolved and imposed on the schools of Europe? For, as we saw earlier, that education was not of a very inspiring sort.

Here again, as with C.S.Lewis's condemnation, a closer look does help. Humanist education means for most of us in the first instance the sort of thing which is described in the Eton *Consuetudinarium*. And justifiably so. The school curricula of the sixteenth century, which have been preserved in quite large numbers [14], were patently intended for just such classroom work as Eton offered. Johann Sturm's programme which served as a model for all Protestant schools sets out the whole business — the same sort of timetable, roughly the same curriculum as we find later at Eton — in the greatest detail, and we come across it afresh in the various educational ordinances produced by the Jesuits [15].

Undoubtedly we have in the *Consuetudinarium* the common pattern of what we call humanist schooling. But — and this is a very large *but* — the pattern was not established until the latter end of the Renaissance. The Jesuit schools belong to the second half of the sixteenth century. Sturm's Strassburg programme appeared in 1537. St Paul's — the earliest humanist foundation in England — perhaps the earliest school of that particular type anywhere — goes back to the century's second decade. Petrarch, Boccaccio, Ficino, Politian, Erasmus himself, Colet, Sir Thomas More — none of these well-known humanists received what we normally call a humanist education. Rabelais was no old Etonian.

So our single problem breaks up into several. We have to ask ourselves how the schooling received by the earlier humanists compared with the schooling established in the sixteenth century. Then, if we find that there was an appreciable change in the pattern of education, we must ask ourselves whether there was any corresponding change in the character of humanism. Did the classical scholars of the counter-reformation period — a Lipsius, a Nizolio or J.J. Scaliger, have the same interests as their fifteenth-century predecessors? Did the writers who came under humanist influence after 1530 — Ronsard who had studied under Dorat at Coqueret, Spencer who had been at Merchant Taylor's, Sidney who had been at Shrewsbury, Montaigne who was educated at the famous humanist college at Bordeaux — draw from that influence the same sort of inspiration as a Boccaccio, a Sannazaro or a Rabelais had done?

Since these questions are interconnected, it will be convenient to begin with the first and to consider the character of the education which the humanist schools replaced.

Georg Voigt's well-known book [16], which served for many years as the one definite history of humanism during the fourteenth and fifteenth centuries, tells us next to nothing about the schools of the day and the way instruction was organized. It is the history of Hamlet without the court of Denmark. And though nearly ninety years have passed since Voigt wrote, we are still far from being able to fill the gaps he left. We are faced with a great variety of small developments, few of which had more than a local importance, and about which we possess very little information. What we have to study is not an ordered system, but something akin to an organic growth of great diversity.

Our starting-point for the study of this growth is the schooling which became popular in the Middle Ages. Of the many oddities which the history of education brings to our notice, this medieval system is perhaps the most bizarre. Children began learning Latin at six or seven. The work they did was language study stripped to its bare essentials, just grammar and the meanings of words, like learning an elaborate code by heart. This took them some six or seven years, and, towards the end of that period, they spent some time mugging up figures of of speech, the lists we find at the end of that least inspired of Roman textbooks, the *Rhetorica ad Herennium*; epanaphora, antistrophe, apostrophe, isocolon, homoioptoton, homoioteleuton, and so forth. These were to be learnt and applied. At twelve or thirteen, they switched over to the study of logic. They struggled with Aristotle's *Categories*, with the various modes of the syllogism, *barbara, celarent, darii, ferioque prioris...* They learnt to construct arguments. They defended and opposed theses propounded by the master. And this logic — the staple of the arts course — occupied them till adolescence. They learnt to reason with extraordinary subtlety but in an intellectual vacuum; for, until they turned at the end of their course to some metaphysics and natural history out of Pliny and Aristotle, logic was all they knew.

A form of education that was so narrow in its scope was bound to drive men to look elsewhere for intellectual training. We have here an example for once of the Marxist principle that a thesis generates its own antithesis. The Latin training of the medieval clerks competed everywhere with a lively vernacular culture — English, French, Italian, Spanish — which people mastered by their own efforts once they had learnt to read. And at the same time, there were types of education available which made use of Latin but steered clear of logic.

The most important of the fringe courses using Latin, that grew up alongside the main grammar-cum-logic curriculum, was *dictamen*, the teaching of letter-writing. This seems to have become established already in the twelfth century as an adjunct to the teaching of law; for it flourished most obviously in the great legal centres of Bologna and Orléans. But its connection with Law was no more than an accidental one. Some of the letters people were likely to want written had admittedly a legal character; but the seven volumes of Buoncampagno's popular *Ars Dictaminis* (1215) [17] contain a great many model letters that are not in any sense legal. How do you address an archbishop? How do you write to an uncle from whom you expect an inheritance when you hear that the government has sent him into exile and confiscated his estates? How do you propose to a rich widow? There were problems of tact as well as problems of law on which the inexperienced needed instruction. The thirteenth century had professional letter-writers to whom men went to have their letters composed as we now go to a solicitor to have a contract drawn up. It also had in increasing numbers its professional clerks who sat in chanceries and drafted official letters for people in authority. They all needed special instruction. Men like Buoncampagno made a fair living out of running courses for them, and these courses in spite of their utilitarian character offered a more broadly based education than the universities with their logic.

At the same time, there are indications already in the thirteenth century that the training in logic was coming to appear over-specialized to men who wanted their sons to take over an estate or a business and who wanted them to acquire just a modicum of literacy and general knowledge. Round about 1300 we find in Italy — at any rate in the Veneto — schools of rhetoric which kept pupils beyond the age when boys normally passed from grammar to logic. They catered, one suspects, for boys who did not then go on to a university. Evidence about the activities of these schools is now being collected by some of Professor Billanovich's pupils [18]. They seem to have had some of the features of the later humanist schools, reading the better-known Latin authors, practising the writing of what was then considered stylish Latin, the florid diction of the chanceries, packed with figures of speech, but style for style's sake nevertheless. These little schools turned out a class whom the educated men of the day no doubt considered semi-educated, but who knew more about subjects like literature and history than the educated did.

Roberto Weiss, whose recent death was a great blow to humanist studies, Renucci, Billanovich and others have shown conclusively that humanism had its roots in these fringe interests of the fourteenth century. The early humanists found their audience among the lawyers, the chancery clerks, the (by the standards of the time) half-educated merchants and gentry of northern Italy. And in the first place the humanist educational programme was limited to winning respect for those desultory studies from which the movement sprang, studies that went under the time-honoured name of rhetoric.

I have used the words educational programme — but programme is altogether too strong a term for this context as far as the fourteenth century is concerned. The early humanists put their trust in the propagandist power of the written word. They had a very poor opinion of what teachers could achieve. Petrarch habitually bewailed the lot of schoolmasters. He thought they had an ill-paid, dull and brutalizing job; and he went to considerable trouble trying to persuade his young friend Zanobi da Strada to give up the school Zanobi had inherited from his father in Florence [19].

Given the educational conditions of the time, this was not an unreasonable attitude. Rhetoric, which could involve the reading of classical authors, was the only teaching subject that offered an opening for a humanist; and rhetoric was taught to young boys. Its teachers were at the bottom of the educational hierarchy.

Arts in the medieval universities was a preparatory course which you took before you got down to the serious business of law, medicine or theology. And the important parts of it were the years spent on logic, metaphysics and natural philosophy. The teacher of grammar and rhetoric with his horde of grubby small boys had no standing at all. He ranked far below the doctors, the theologians, the highly skilled civilians and canonists. It was not the sort of job that an ambitious man would want to take.

But although the humanists were initially uninterested in teaching, their propaganda during the fourteenth century did work a change. To start with, humanist aspirations had the effect of making rhetoric teachers more ambitious. Bruno Casini, a contemporary of Petrarch, who had a school in Florence, taught his pupils to declaim in Latin and was famous for the show he put on with them. He organized what were speech days in the strict sense of the word [20]. And at the same time, the new ideas on style popularized by the humanists also had the effect of making the rhetoric teacher's educational role more important. You can teach a boy to use the rhetorical figures of the *Ad Herennium* inside a few weeks. But training him to write good classical Latin takes years. Inculcate a taste for the imitation of Cicero and you provide substantial employment for those who can teach Ciceronian Latin. Another humanist innovation which again had the effect of raising the status of the rhetoric teacher was the cult of Greek. Greek had no place in the curriculum. It was a modish extra, and its professors initially at least could command a fair salary; and even later, when the knowledge of Greek became more common, an offer to teach it alongside rhetoric had sometimes the effect of putting the rhetoric teacher in a higher income-bracket.

We have a few figures which can illustrate this situation. An eminent jurist in the fifteenth century could earn 600 to 800 *scudi* a year. Valla as professor of rhetoric at Pavia at the beginning of his career was offered 50 *scudi*. An undistinguished humanist like Lauro Quirino had to be content at Bologna with 40 *ducats* which was a tenth of what the law professor was paid. On the other hand Manuel Chrysoloras was offered 250 florins when he became professor of Greek at Florence. The florin was worth more than the *scudo*, so this is a middling good salary. Filelfo a quarter of a century later commanded 450 *scudi* at Bologna, and in 1455 Florence was offering 400 florins. Eventually, by combining rhetoric and Greek, men like Guarino, Filelfo, Marsuppini, humanists at the top of their profession, managed to earn a reasonable livelihood. But the majority of their kind were ill paid [21].

We must also bear in mind that humanist studies, whether in Greek or rhetoric, remained extra-curricular, except for the very elementary rhetoric that was taught to boys at school. Your humanist lecturer was concerned to interest his audience. Making sure that his pupils learnt something was not part of his task. Politian in the 1480s enlivened his lectures on ancient authors by the impassioned declamation of poems he had composed on the subject of his course, a trick which won him an audience but was unlikely to have been very informative [22].

Humanist education in the fifteenth century operated therefore at several levels. We come across a small body of well-known professors whose teaching activity was largely aimed at arousing a general interest in the classical past and was an adjunct to their activity as writers. Then we have a few — but only a few — teachers like Guarino and Vittorino da Feltre, who ran private schools attended mostly by the very rich. Their pupils did get a very thorough knowledge of classical Latin and ancient literature. But they were a tiny minority. Finally, far below these in esteem and atrociously paid, we have the ordinary schoolmasters and letter-writing masters who taught substantial numbers, and who seem to have carried on much as their predecessors had done in the Middle Ages. They, and they alone, served the majority. But what standard did they reach?

North of the Alps, the picture is fairly clear. Up to the time when Erasmus came on the scene at the end of the fifteenth century, the teaching of Latin remained much as it had been two hundred years earlier. The Institute for Renaissance and Humanist Studies in Brussels and the Seminarium Philologiae Humanisticae at Louvain have been producing a great deal of material lately on the immediate predecessors of Erasmus, and it is fast becoming plain that these so-called prehumanists of the Netherlands did little more than tinker with the educational practices of the Middle Ages. Up to 1490 at any rate, they used the old medieval grammars, and their idea of style was still to heap up as many figures of speech as possible. Their popular new textbook for letter-writing, produced by a certain Carolus Meneken, included a few model letters by Petrarch and Aeneas Sylvius but otherwise followed the formulas invented during the thirteenth century [23]. In England there seems to have been a great shortage of grammar teachers in the middle of the fifteenth century because the job was so badly rewarded; and such grammar as was taught had nothing humanist about it. We find in Bale an account of a certain Galfridus Grammaticus who flourished round 1460: 'In his lessons he despised Cicero, Vergil and other good authors and instead made use of that ruin of the Latin tongue and nausea of good wits, the sordid and horrible dregs of Alexander, Garlande, Johannes Balbus Januensis and the like' [24].

Bale was a self-righteous mid-sixteenth-century humanist, but he makes his point. A hundred years before his time there was nothing in England remotely resembling a humanist school. And the same was true of France, where we find, as late as 1530, Mathurin Cordier giving examples of the kind of Latin boys talked at school: *est totum* (*c'est tout*), French in Latin words.

But of course there was not much by way of humanist culture or Renaissance ideas in either of these northern countries before 1490. So our real problem is with Italy, and there the picture is just as confused for the fifteenth century as it was for the fourteenth.

I mentioned earlier that the first generations of humanists had little interest in what was taught in schools, and one consequence of this disinterest was a lack of humanist grammars and other teaching books which lasted until the middle of the fifteenth century. The appearance of Lorenzo Valla's *Elegantiae*, which drew attention to the niceties of Latin style and the errors of previous grammarians, was the real watershed between the old world and the new. It was composed during the last twenty years of his life; but did not become really famous until the first printed edition of 1471, fourteen years after his death. Valla's work was followed by a spate of humanist grammars, and it is reasonable to suppose that some of these at least were used in the schools. But we must note that printers continued to push out the medieval grammar in even larger numbers. And we must also take into account the time which must elapse before the results of an educational system can be observed. If teaching in schools did improve in Italy — or shall we say became more humanist — during the twenty years between 1460 and 1480, we are unlikely to be able to trace the effects of this in literature and general culture much before 1500.

In short, that flowering of the Renaissance which was responsible for for most of what is valuable in neo-Latin literature, for the first triumphs of classical scholarships and astronomy, for the revival of Platonism, for painters like Leonardo and Botticelli, for writers like Petrarch, Boccaccio, Boiardo, Cosimo de' Medici and Rabelais — this sweeping cultural advance which had undoubted connections with a love of the Greek and Roman past — was a product of *avant-garde* enthusiasm and owed little or nothing to the general education of the time. Classical borrowings played a dynamic role. They served as a jumping-off ground for invention. Boccaccio and Sannazaro took Virgil's idealization of country life and linking it with mythology and romance created the pastoral novel. Ariosto, working somewhat later but in the same tradition, produced the romantic epic. Ficino's Platonic theology built a great imaginative superstructure on Plato's teaching. What occurred seems to confirm the dictum that minds are like parachutes. They work only if they are open. The lack of any systematic training left these men of the early Renaissance with open minds in which the humanist seed, casually implanted, had room to grow.

The world was transformed without the help of systematic education. But did the humanist education when it came then achieve nothing? Before we say so, we must take a look at the other side of the picture, the achievements of the second half of the sixteenth century. The humanists obtained control of the schools and arts teaching in the universities between 1520 and 1560 — in England, France, Germany and last of all with the Jesuits in Italy. During these years and the decades that followed, science continued to advance, painters continued to paint, the new literatures brought forth fresh masterpieces. Tasso, Guarini, Ronsard and Montaigne, Spenser, Marlowe, Shakespeare, Bacon, Jonson, Cervantes, all belong to the age when schoolboys were made to read their classical authors and to practise writing Latin themes after the manner of Cicero; and we must now consider how this later Renaissance differed from its predecessor, and if the differences (such as they were) can be traced to the educational change that had taken place.

These are not questions which it would be easy to answer even if our knowledge was much fuller and better organized than it is. All one can do is to point out the problems involved and perhaps hazard the shadow of a guess. The first difficulty is that the later Renaissance was a continuation of the earlier. The men of the sixteenth century built on what the men of the fifteenth had achieved. This is certainly true of painting, which after 1500 developed under its own impetus. In architecture, one can perhaps trace with Palladio an exactitude in the rendering of classical detail which one fails to find in Bramante; and one could link this at a pinch with a general leaning towards more exact study of the past. In the sciences, certain classical authors were usefully studied, authors whom the fifteenth century had not plumbed — Dioscorides for botany, Nicomachus of Gerasa in mathematics. But if humanism contributed to such learning, it was through the textual scholarship which had developed before 1500 making the authors in question available to all. We are left therefore with literature, but here again a large group of writers, notably in the epic and pastoral conventions (Ariosto, Spenser, Montemayor, Sidney in the *Arcadia*, Cervantes in his pastoral *Galatea*), are deeply indebted to their immediate Latin and Italian predecessors; and one feels they would have written as they did whatever their education. We have continuities of development which make the influence of contemporary schooling very hard to assess.

A further and somewhat kindred difficulty is that not every student who attended a humanist school carried away with him the stamp of its training. Montaigne confessed that he left the École de Guyenne a worse Latinist than he had been when he entered it. And everybody knows about Shakespeare's small Latin. If these men owed a debt to the classics, it was a debt independent of their training; and it is notable that they both use classical material in the dynamic way which had been popular at earlier age.

If we are to look for an observable difference between our two periods, it must be with writers like the French Pléiade, Ben Jonson and Bacon, who were more precisely the products of the conditions of their own times. And what is noticeable with these writers is a certain absence of dynamism in their borrowing. They do not build freely on what they borrow. Their minds are dominated by the conventions of the genre in which they have chosen to write, and they borrow principally what had belonged to that context in antiquity. Bacon admittedly falls outside this generalization for he does not write in an ancient genre. But again his main debt to the past is structural. It is shown by the way he organizes his arguments according to the principles of rhetorical partition, by the way in which he uses illustrations and apophthegms in argument, by his respect, in appropriate contexts, for the syllogism [25]. The sixteenth century at its close was already moving towards that respect for rules which soon after found its fullest expression in the French classical drama.

And here tenuously one does glimpse a possible link with the aims of the humanist education. At the beginning of this paper I described the classroom face of that education in a manner which emphasized its narrowness and dullness. I must now say something about it along more general lines. Look at it in detail, and you find that everything leads up to the writing of Latin themes. The language was learnt from the beginning actively rather than passively. When a passage had been read and explained, the next stage was always to memorize its more elegant phrases for use in other contexts. Erasmus in his *De Copia Verborum ac Rerum* had recommended the keeping of two notebooks by every scholar. In the first he was to write down vocabulary, figures of speech, neat expressions; in the other, he was to collect anecdotes, historical instances, pregnant generalizations. *Copia* — abundance of material — was the key concept. The student was to have as many ways as possible of expressing an idea. Erasmus began one of his colloquies by listing some twenty phrases which you could use for greeting a friend you met in the street. And this *copia*, this stock of material, embraced not only expression, but also subject-matter. Given a topic — honour, ingratitude, the horrors of war — your fully trained humanist had ready a dozen stock stories, a dozen stock generalizations to illustrate it.

This is a view of the art of writing which is very different from our own, and the idea that one can be trained to write in this way has some strange implications. It presupposes first of all that the number of topics on which one wants to write is limited. The student can cover the whole ground. Secondly it presupposes that what one wants to say on each topic is a repetition of what has been said before, or at best a recombination of previously used elements. Here is a view of writing that leaves much less scope for originality and self-expression than we consider necessary nowadays. It also leaves less scope for a direct notation of experience. The greatest part of the material a writer uses is predigested literary stuff.

We have in the school theme and the methods recommended for producing it an explanation of that lifeless, conventional quality which marks so much of late humanist writing.

And there remains a further point to add. In the more efficient schools, the prose theme or essay was not the final product. Boys learnt to write elegies, satires, epic passages, odes in verse. At the universities, they tried their hand at comedy and tragedy. They were made aware of the differences between genres. And according to the critical theories of the humanists, each genre, each literary kind that is, had its particular structure, its style and subject-matter. Here again as with the general topics I mentioned above, the writer's task was envisaged as the working out of a traditional pattern, whose strict framework restricted original invention. The formalism we have noticed in the literature of this period was also to be found in its schools.

What a cursory examination of the facts suggests is that the only contribution the humanist schools are likely to have made to the development of European literature was to have accentuated its tendency to formalism. If they helped at all, they helped the evolution of literary kinds like the Miltonian epic and the French classical drama. We are back therefore to C.S.Lewis's taunt about *Gorboducs*, which we now see have been directed not at the whole of humanism, but at its later manifestations. Leave the formal genres to one side, and the progress of literature, science and the arts during the three centuries of the Renaissance can be recognized as due to self-education. If the schools had a role, it was a preparatory one. By guaranteeing a minimum of literacy and intellectual interest, they created an environment in which self-education could flourish. In the fifteenth century generally and in the less efficient schools of the sixteenth, enough education was given to make the young responsive to the ideas and literary experiments of the time but they did not receive the kind of rigorous and extensive training which could have made them cherish specific values or look at the universe in some specific way; and the formula would seem to have worked. A little learning was not a dangerous thing. In this age at least, it was the precondition of progress.

# Notes

[1] A medallion by Pisanello dating from before 1450 and representing P.P.Decembrio carries the inscription *studiorum humanitatis decus*. But no one could have equated the activities of Decembrio, who was a Papal Secretary, a historian and a translator of Plato, with the teaching of grammar. It follows therefore that *humanitas* had a wider connotation by the middle of the fifteenth century.

[2] C.S.Lewis, *English Literature in the Sixteenth Century* (Oxford, 1954), p.2.

[3] Ibid., p.19.

[4] Ibid., p.31.

[5] A translation of P.P.Vergerio's *De Ingenuis Moribus* can be found in W.H.Woodward, *Vittorino da Feltre and other Humanist Educators* (Cambridge, 1897).

[6] Roger Ascham's *The Scholemaster* (1570) has been edited in the original spelling by W.A.Wright (Cambridge English Classics, 1904).

[7] The *Consuetudinarium Scholae Etonensis,* probably the work of William Malim who was Headmaster in 1560, has been printed in H.C.Maxwell Lyte, *The History of Eton College* (London, 1875), chap.vii.

[8] For an attempt to work out how much time was spent on the reading of classical authors, see R.R.Bolgar, 'Classical Reading in Renaissance Schools', *Durham Research Review*, No.6 (1955), pp. 18–26.

[9] J.Sturm, *De Litterarum Ludis Recte Aperiendis* (Strassburg, 1537).

[10] G.Billanovich, 'Petrarch and the Textual Tradition of Livy', *Journal of the Warburg and Courtauld Institutes,* vol.xiv (1951), pp. 137–208.

[11] J.E.Sandys, *A History of Classical Scholarship* (3 vols.) (Cambridge, 1903–8).

[12] M.Manitius, *Geschichte der lateinischen Literatur des Mittelalters* (3 vols.) (Munich, 1911–30).

[13] For the development of the Dido story in the Romance languages see E.Leube, *Fortuna in Karthago* (Heidelberg, 1969).

[14] T.W.Baldwin, *William Shakespeare's 'Small Latin and Lesse Greeke'* (Urbana, Ill., 1944).

[15] For an analysis of the various Jesuit *Rationes Studiorum* see A.P.Farrell, *The Jesuit Code of Liberal Education* (Milwaukee, 1938).

[16] G.Voigt, *Die Wiederbelebung des classischen Alterthums* (2 vols.) (Berlin, 1879).

[17] C.H.Haskins, *Studies in Medieval Culture* (Oxford, 1929), p.170.

[18] L.Gargan, 'Oliviero Forzetta e la diffusione dei testi classici nel Veneto', in R.R.Bolgar (ed.), *Classical Influences on European Culture 500–1500* (Cambridge, 1971).

[19] Petrarch *Epist.Rer.Famil.* xii.3.

[20] Filippo Villani, *Liber de Famosis Civibus*, ed. G.C.Galletti (Florence, 1847), p.30.

[21] R.R.Bolgar 'Provision for Education in the Free Cities of Italy', *Year Book of Education 1955*, pp. 118–129.

[22] J.E.Sandys, op.cit., II, 84.

[23] A.Gerlo 'Erasmus's treatise on letter-writing: its background and influence' in R.R.Bolgar (ed.), op.cit.

[24] Foster Watson, *The English Grammar Schools to 1660* (Cambridge, 1908), pp. 229–30.

[25] B.W.Vickers, *Francis Bacon and Renaissance Prose* (Cambridge, 1968).

CHARLES WEBSTER

# Science and the challenge to the scholastic curriculum 1640-1660

'The end then of learning is to repair the ruins of our first parents by regaining to know God aright.' So opened Milton's tract, *On Education*, the most famous educational work of the Puritan revolution. In emphasizing the primacy of the religious goal in life, Milton was expressing a priority which would have been universally acknowledged by his contemporaries. To the head of family or minister in his parish, the main educational agents of this period, the primary concern was imparting literacy for the purpose of scriptural appreciation and religious exercise. Generally, prior to the Puritan revolution, there had been little concern to extend the educational horizon of the majority of the population. Only for the higher ranks of society had secular education come to fulfil an important role, the private tutor or grammar school providing a grounding in classical language and the liberal arts, which were studied more exhaustively in the universities. This pattern became increasingly popular in the sixteenth century as a general education for the gentry as well as being the basis for higher professional studies.

Since the Renaissance most educational writings had been concerned with the perfection of the liberal arts curriculum, the details of which became enshrined in the statutes of the humanist schools and universities. While the ultimate religious aims of the scholastic curriculum were not in doubt, the *pietas literata* was approached through grammars, logics and classical texts having only the remotest relationship to reformed Protestantism.

In the seventeenth century there was increasing dissatisfaction with this educational order, criticisms reaching a peak during the Puritan revolution, during pressure for complete reconstruction of the church and social institutions. This wave of enthusiasm for social experiment, given ample room for expression by the collapse of press censorship, far outstripped the interests, financial resources and legislative abilities of the interregnum governments. However, reform proposals proliferated, their advocates being strengthened by a belief in the imminent achievement of a utopian state. This millenary spirit imparted a sense of urgency as well as encouraging radical ideas.

This atmosphere evoked a re-examination of all aspects of education, with the aim of ensuring that all would make the maximum use of their capacities in the new spiritual and social order. The existing educational provisions were recognized as totally inadequate for this end. The lower classes were insufficiently educated, while the sophisticated humanistic education was inappropriate for the times. Traditionally it had been assumed that the mechanic and agricultural labourer had no need of formal education to assist his vocation, while the minister, lawyer and physician required the scholastic university training. Now the more radical thinkers suggested that education might greatly assist the mechanic, while the professions were hindered by their scholastic equipment. With this reversal of traditional values, no institutions were sacrosanct. Reformers called for a complete recasting of the educational system in accordance with new ideas on social role and intellectual capacity, which were greatly influenced by the growing scientific tradition of the seventeenth century.

In religious motivation the reformers of the Puritan revolution had strong links with the Reformation. Experimental science was a new factor in the intellectual situation. In their various spheres of interest, Gilbert, Galileo, Kepler and Harvey illustrated the inadequacy of natural philosophy inherited from antiquity and the fertility of systematic observation and controlled experiment as a means to the understanding and control of the environment. Descartes quickly developed a system of mechanical philosophy which assimilated these new scientific currents, thus creating a vehicle whereby the new science could challenge traditional natural philosophy in the higher education context. Finally, Francis Bacon, although himself with an uncertain knowledge of these scientific trends, became the scientific movement's most effective publicist. He presented the inductive methods of experimental science as a model for the progress of all branches of learning. To Bacon, the educational reformers of the Renaissance, such as Sturm and Ascham, had successfully emancipated language from the barbarities of the medieval scholastics, but had deflected learning in the wrong direction, towards eloquence and stylistic perfection, the study of words rather than matter [1]. Each branch of knowledge had merely glided over the surface of its subject because of failure to draw lessons from its root, natural philosophy. This subject was neglected, being treated as an ancillary to a limited range of topics, whereas there would be no progress unless 'natural philosophy be carried on and applied to particular sciences, and particular sciences be carried back again to natural philosophy' [2]. By turning to the study of nature, man would find 'a rich storehouse for the glory of the Creator and the relief of man's estate' [3]. Experimental philosophy was therefore an important aid to material and spiritual regeneration, the key to the reform of scholastic education and the basis for educational provisions for all classes.

As an ordered and systematic exploration of the 'Book of Nature', science had an explicitly religious purpose, providing evidence for the existence and nature of God. As the key to restoring man's dominion over nature through discoveries in technology, agriculture and medicine, science could assume a valuable social role. Thus science could be justified on theological and utilitarian grounds. Both were appealing to the seventeenth-century Puritan, although without Bacon's emphasis on their interdependence. Bacon argued that practical activity would be uncongenial to the philosopher, but it was as necessary for natural philosophy to apply itself to works as it was to prove faith by good works. Consequently, it was illegitimate to separate the theoretical and applied aspects of science. It was not until theories were applied to the test of 'fruits and works' that their truth could be assessed.

Bacon's philosophical programme was readily assimilated into the social and religious outlook of the reformers during the Puritan revolution. The 'advancement of learning' became inextricably linked with the platform for religious reform. The blueprint for the development of secular knowledge was provided by Bacon's *De Augmentis Scientiarum* (1623), which appeared in a lavish English edition, translated by Gilbert Watts in 1640, *Of the Advancement and Proficience of Learning*. Although there was wide acceptance of the value of science, there were sharp differences of outlook about its role in education. The moderates continued to place considerable emphasis on the classical languages, logic and rhetoric for the correct understanding of the scriptures. However, with their increasing attention to natural theology, the sciences became a valued ancillary study. More radical thinkers pronounced the worthlessness of liberal arts for the understanding of the scriptures. Religion was preserved for the individual contemplation of the scriptures aided only by the light of divine revelation. Consequently, formal education could be conducted according to a curriculum based entirely on secular and utilitarian considerations. Hence both parties favoured science, but for very different reasons. To the liberal theologians science was to be propagated because of its obviously theological end, whereas it was acceptable to the radicals because of its theological neutrality and relevance to practical life. This led to strikingly different conceptions of science among its various advocates.

Reconciliation between the rival claims of language and scientific studies was the aim of Jan Amos Comenius, the Czech thinker who formed important links with England in the decade before the civil wars. Starting from the rather unpromising Renaissance 'pansophist' position, Comenius incorporated many of Bacon's ideas in his educational programme. Bacon himself had been content with scattered and general aphorisms about education, with the exception of his plan for an ideal scientific institution, Solomon's House. Comenius's early writings, discussions of educational principles and language textbooks, provided an ideal pedagogical complement to Bacon's philosophical work. His *Janua Linguarum Reserata* (1631), a non-grammatical method of teaching languages, was a considerable success. This book achieved much more than the facilitation of the teaching of classical languages. In particular language was no longer primarily seen as a vehicle to classical literature and the liberal arts. It was the means to pansophia, or universal knowledge. Comenius's method was defined as 'the art of readily, and solidly teaching all men all things' [4]. With the pansophic aim in mind, language would no longer be a harsh discipline. By turning to Nature the student would find:

> A delightful method, temp'ring every where pleasance with profit, and exposing all things to the cleare light, whereby this Amphitheater of the Universe may seem to none a labyrinth or thorny bush, but a Paradice and delicious Garden to all. [5]

Like Bacon, Comenius also reflected on the worthlessness of knowledge divorced from the needs of human life and society.

These priorities were apparent in the *Janua Linguarum*, which provided an ordered description of nature and social organization. It was intended that this should be as far as possible accompanied by practical experience, a point which was re-emphasized in his pioneer illustrated school book, the *Orbis Pictus* (1658).

The English editors of Comenius fully exploited his aim to provide a compendious view of nature during language learning, even to the point of obscuring the simplicity of the original design. The thousand sentences constituting the work became somewhat overburdened with information relating to every sphere of economic life. Sentence 134 had originally listed 20 grassland plants; the 1650 English edition gave 39. The following two sentences catalogued 28 species of culinary herbs and nearly one hundred medicinal plants. In such a scheme the complexities of language structure were largely lost from sight.

Comenius's schoolbooks provided an ideal educational complement to Bacon's natural philosophy. Baconian ideas were again prominent in Comenius's first pansophic writings, which were published by Hartlib at Oxford in 1637, being translated as *A Reformation of Schooles* (1642). Hartlib, a Prussian who had settled in England shortly after the death of Bacon in 1628, became the focus of the educational endeavour during the Puritan revolution. Comenius and Bacon provided the foundations for the programme which Hartlib and his associates attempted to translate into practical terms. Education of the whole community had the first priority: 'For, all things being rightly weighed, we shall perceive that this Endeavour alone, or nothing, will be able to work a reformation in this our Age' [6].

Hartlib's initial aim was to establish, on the model described in *De Augmentis Scientiarum*, a collegiate society of scholars who would advance learning and settle religious disputes. They would then supervise the reform of the nation's social institutions, particularly education. Comenius was the natural head of this *collegium lucis*. Convinced that these schemes had parliamentary sanction, he was persuaded to visit England in 1641, when parliamentary patronage of the project seemed likely. Although this dreamed-of *collegium lucis* was never formally established, Hartlib was tireless in his efforts to induce parliament to adopt a constructive social programme. In particular, he was active in inducing his numerous associates to elaborate reform projects which were duly presented to parliament. Educational reform was a dominant interest, Hartlib being associated in some way with the celebrated writings of Comenius, Dury, Milton, Petty and Woodward, as well as a number of lesser-known published and unpublished tracts on education. Outside the Hartlib circle similar themes were developed by other writers, though generally in a more polemical vein, which was alien to Hartlib.

This literature, representing many different points of view, indicates the great pressure for parliamentary intervention in education, with the aim of providing extensive formal education for all classes. This was a demand which united Samuel Harmar's *Vox Populi: Gloucestershire's Desire* (1642), the Hartlib circle, the Levellers and Gerrard Winstanley. On the matter of curriculum in reformed education one of the most prevalent demands was for increased recognition of experimental science. Existing educational institutions were criticized for indifference to the recent efflorescence in science. Science became a central feature in the plans for new educational institutions for all social classes.

There was a new vitality in plans for the education of the lower classes. The priority of the religious goal of education was still paramount. William Dell advocated the provision of schools to 'bring them to *read* the HOLY SCRIPTURES, which though for the present they understand not, yet may they (through the blessing of God) come to understand them afterwards' [7]. Such reformers as Dell and Winstanley were well aware that the transference of educational obligation from the minister to the magistrate would greatly enhance individual responsibility in religious matters and free congregations from the dominance of the learned ministry. With this recognition of the worth of the religious experience of the simple man, or *idiota*, there came a greater respect for his skills and practical knowledge. Winstanley suggested that the intuitive skills of the manual labourer presented the soundest foundations for knowledge, a point of view shared by Bacon and Comenius, who contrasted the sterility of scholastic learning with the healthy state of the mechanical arts, from which had emerged inventions with the capacity to revolutionize Western society. In addition, Comenius pointed out that the mechanic was free from the moral corruption which was instilled by the study of 'Heathenish Phylosophy'. Ideally, the mechanical arts were a model of knowledge accumulated by a method involving moral integrity and were thus 'endued with vitall spirit, encrease dayly, and come to perfection' [8].

In designing the educational programme for the lower classes, the reformers sought to build naturally upon their intrinsic skills, rather than imitate elements of the scholastic curriculum. It was felt that this approach was educationally sound, and would also arrest the economic decline of the Civil War period and assist in solving the problems of poverty and unemployment. Hartlib's emphasis was on poor-law reform, projecting a national system of workhouses which would provide basic education and craft training for the poor, whose employment would be organized by labour exchanges, an aspect of his Office of Address project.

In extensive proposals addressed to the Saints' Parliament in 1653, Hartlib and Dury urged that the provision of common and mechanical schools should be a first social priority [9]. Common schools would provide a basic education consisting of reading, writing, arithmetic, geography, secular and religious history, the principles of reasoning and law. The pupil would then proceed to a mechanical school for vocational training. By this means they were confident that 'in a few years the generation of common man in this Commonwealth will be so changed that few commoners in the world, or none in any Nation will be found like unto them for public usefulnesses' [10].

Their associate, William Petty, advocated formal education for all children above seven in *'Ergastrula literaria,* literary work-houses' [11]. As in Hartlib's workhouses the poor would be self-supporting by the products of their manual skill. Petty emphasized the psychological theory evolved in pre-Civil-War days by Comenius and Hartlib. Preparatory to formal literacy, the child was to have the maximum range of sensory experience, this being assisted by drawing. The basic education was even more varied than that proposed by Dury, including an introduction to ideal languages, physical exercises and music. Again this was to be followed by craft instruction, a minority of gifted craftsmen being transferred to other institutions to advance and codify their art in a collegiate atmosphere, their status being similar to that of fellows of colleges at the universities.

A similarly extensive system of education was envisaged in Winstanley's communes [12]. Here the life span was divided into four stages, the first two, childhood and youth, the educative phases, ending at the age of forty. One of the four Overseers of Winstanley's ideal community was to supervise education, that 'the young people may learn the inward knowledg of the things which are, and find out the secrets of nature' [13]. Like Dell, he had an aversion to purely theoretical knowledge, championing the 'actor' against the 'contemplator'. No members of his community would be allowed to possess purely theoretical skills, all being referred to 'bodily action, for the encrease of fruitfulness, freedom and peace in the Earth'. As in the previous examples, a general introductory education was to be followed by vocational training, the sabbath being used for lectures on scientific and historical subjects, designed to improve the community's knowledge of astronomy, navigation, medicine and husbandry [14].

These proposals for the extension of lower-class education show a strikingly fresh approach, owing little to existing educational structures and traditions. The educational ideals evolved by Bacon and Comenius seemed naturally applicable to a social class which could exploit experimental knowledge in daily life. It was difficult to give the same sense of relevance of a scientifically based education to the higher ranks of society, accustomed to the virtuous or noble education evolved by the Renaissance humanists. This education seemed ideally suited to the courtly life to which they aspired. In essence natural philosophy and mathematics could play an important role in the humanistic programme; it was even tolerant of the experimental approach. But in practice, by the mid-seventeenth century, there had developed a considerable gulf between the scholastic physics and mathematics and the mathematics and physics of the practising scientist. Even more seriously for the community, after Harvey and Paracelsus, the obsolete nature of

Galenic medicine was becoming apparent.

These defects are clear with hindsight, but they were not apparent to the schools and universities during the Puritan revolution. The reformers received little sympathy, but this did not deter their onslaught against the scholastic curriculum.

Bacon and Comenius had provided the philosophical and psychological grounds for arguments against the scholastic curriculum, suggesting a reversal of the traditional order of education to emphasize the 'sciences' rather than the 'arts' of traditional studies. This would place emphasis on the expansion of knowledge rather than perfection of literary expression. Bacon's favourite image for the scholastic was of the spider weaving webs of sophistry from its own body. Even more popular was the parrot, with an endless capacity for conversation but with no understanding. *Res et verba* was the theme of the reformers, all eloquence and logic being subservient to the ideal of the economical use of language to convey objective information. Dury argued 'that the teaching of words is no further usefull than the things signified therby are familiar to the Imagination' [15]. Similarly John Hall; it was 'better to grave *things* on the mindes of children than *words*' [16]. This was the aim of Comenius's language teaching, the method of *precognita* evolved by the Hartlib circle, the stimulus to the study of universal language, and was finally embodied in the philosophical programme of the Royal Society. Its historian, Thomas Sprat, expressed this aim:

> to return back to the primitive purity and shortness, when men delivered so many *things,* almost in an equal number of *words.* They have exacted from all their members, a close, naked, natural way of speaking; positive expressions; clear senses; a native easiness: bringing all things as near the Mathematical plainness, as they can: and preferring the language of Artizans, Countrymen, and Merchants, before that of Wits, or Scholars [17].

The programme for the reformed commonwealth recognized the necessity of creating a new image for the gentry, emphasizing participation in the economic life, rather than courtly status. Much of the reformers' effort was spent on urging the social necessity and individual profitability of studies which had hitherto been thought appropriate for the lower classes. Many went further and would enforce this policy as a means of levelling the community. Petty's literary workhouses were intended for all classes 'though of the highest rank' aiming to deflect the nobleman from the traditional 'ignoble, unnecessary, or condemned' parts of learning [18]. With this education they would be less easily cheated by craftsmen, could undertake and supervise many practical tasks themselves, with subsequent saving of wages and potential profit from inventions. As gentlemen, their pride would prompt them to excel much to the advantage of the republic of arts. With these new interests they would become patrons of the mechanical arts. In a project complementary to Petty's, another of Hartlib's protégés, Cressy Dymock, encouraged the gentry to improve their farming techniques by apprenticing their sons at a college of husbandry [19].

One of the most substantial and significant educational works of this period was Dury's *The Reformed School* (1650). Here Dury, probably following the genre established by Milton, described an academy for youths between the ages of eight and twenty. Dury carried much further the drift away from the scholastic education, already detectable in Milton. Languages were necessary, but only as a means of conveying information not attainable directly. His maxim was 'Arts or Sciences which may be received by meer Sense should not be taught any other way' [20]. The aim of this education was to provide detailed knowledge on the 'state of Husbandry, in necessary Trades, in Navigation, in Civill Offices for the administration of Justice' [21]. In the final stage of this education, comparable to normal undergraduate studies, the student would complete his studies in agriculture, natural history, architecture, navigation, moral philosophy, economics, law, mathematics, natural philosophy, medicine and history. The traditional undergraduate topics, logic and rhetoric, occupied less than one-tenth of this course. As far as possible, Dury reduced each topic to a form which would be taught in a graduated manner to suit each stage of psychological development.

If fulfilled, Dury's elaborate plan would have left little scope for recreation or aesthetic pleasures. In the interests of public service, it would have demanded great discipline and self-sacrifice from teachers and students alike.

Other projectors, inspired with a more dilettante interest in science and following the example of the continental gentlemen's academies, proposed courses of study paying considerable attention to science as a novel gentlemanly diversion. The adventurer, Sir Balthazar Gerbier, made ostentatious claims for such an academy at Bethnal Green [22]. William Sprigge writing on behalf of the younger sons, campaigned for a national system of such colleges, which would introduce the sciences in company with the riding of the great horse, vaulting, fencing, etc. [23]. A more serious and interesting scheme for a scientific academy came from the poet Abraham Cowley. This was composed in about 1658, but not published until the Restoration [24]. Cowley regretted that university education was based exclusively on the arts 'intirely spun out of himself', paying too little attention to the 'Inquisition into the Nature of Gods Creatures, and Application of them to Humane uses...' [25]. This neglect could be repaired by establishing a Philosophical College near London, lavishly endowed to enable twenty philosophers to research and teach pupils in an adjacent school. This college would have fulfilled the research functions of Bacon's Solomon's House, while imparting an education not unlike that of *The Reformed School*.

All the educational projects discussed so far were basically new ventures intended to rival or complement the existing educational foundations. None had more than an ephemeral existence. As would be expected, the reformers were extremely critical of the universities and grammar schools, but seem to have taken little interest in reforming the latter. Their attention focused on the symbols of scholastic influence, the universities, which had been susceptible to parliamentary interference after falling into parliamentary hands during the Civil Wars. Reformers attempted to provoke parliament to act on its commitment to university reform which had been stated in 1641. Action was dramatic, but it was confined mainly to sweeping changes in personnel. John Hall complained that the changes had only political significance and had possibly reduced scholarly standards [26]. Parliamentary influence was not applied to modify the Elizabethan and Laudian statutes governing academic practices in the universities. This inaction was probably encouraged by the general complacency of the intruded academics, who showed exemplary respect for the codes compiled by their former persecutor, Archbishop Laud. With the exception of William Dell, most of the pressure for university reform came from outside, where proposals ranged from reform to abolition. Moderate and radical opinion was united in a desire to abandon the scholastic curriculum, introduce studies more relevant to social needs and provide university-level education in major provincial centres.

Lack of sympathy for these aims within the universities is somewhat surprising since the intruded academics included many advocates of experimental science, particularly at Oxford in the circle around John Wilkins at Wadham College. Within a decade this group was to form a substantial basis for the foundation of the Royal Society.

Impatient critics accused the universities of maintaining monkish aloofness from the social needs of the nation, while failing to take account of the fertile intellectual developments of the seventeenth century. There were numerous demands for curricular changes to reflect a more positive attitude to knowledge. Commonly advocated substitutes for the liberal arts included:

(a) Mathematics and the practical disciplines associated with it.
(b) Practical medical education through dissection, vivisection and botany.
(c) Chemistry, which Hall described as 'having snatcht the Keyes of Nature for other sects of Philosophy' [27].
(d) A full consideration of ancient and modern philosophical systems, including experimental philosophy.

The opinions came from various sources — the writings of Dury and Hartlib, a manifesto presented to parliament by their Oxford friends [28], John Hall's *Humble Motion* to parliament based on experience at Cambridge, but the most detailed and polemical attack came from John Webster, in his *Examen Academiarum: An Examination of the Academies* (1654).

Webster's forthright, but ill-digested pamphlet was singled out by Wilkins and Ward as their target in a defence of the universities, *Vindiciae Academiarum* (1654). Webster was easy meat for the skilled dialectician who went systematically through the book indicating his ignorance of the state of knowledge at Oxford and their own superior scientific abilities. However, their clever, pungent satire skilfully avoided the central issue of curricular change, for Webster and other critics pressed for a complete reconstruction of the formal university studies, not the informal provision of modern subjects at the discretion of *avant-garde* academics. Undoubtedly Webster underestimated the scientific movement at Oxford, but the claim that students could obtain adequate guidance on scientific matters carried no implication that this enlightened education should be systematically available, or that its statutory recognition was necessary.

The two sides were arguing at cross-purposes. Looking forward to a period of great social change, the reformers sought to modify the university curriculum in accordance with the ideals of the new society. As a contrast, Wilkins and Ward regarded it as the primary obligation of the universities to fulfil their traditional social role. They admitted the general desirability of introducing agriculture, mechanics and chemistry into university studies, if the primary concern was the perfection of natural philosophy. However, the nobility and gentry required not the sciences, but 'that their reason, and fancy, and carriage, be improved by lighter Institutions and Exercises, that they may become Rationall and Gracefull speakers, and be of an acceptable behaviour in their countries' [29]. Given the option, not one per cent of the students would select the demanding study of natural philosophy.

With their knowledge of the rapidly advancing and fluctuating world of the physical sciences and mathematics, the Oxford circle came to regard science as a subject apart from the fixed body of knowledge, which was the province of scholastic education. It was therefore more suited to mature scholars, gifted individuals and private societies, such as the group meeting at Oxford during the Interregnum. With this outlook, science was not a suitable substitute for traditional studies; it was not cultivated for its social applicability; finally, its sophistication rendered it unsuitable for the lower classes. The most suitable means for its advancement was the constitution of well-endowed private societies which could support the activities of select groups of scholars, who would be given technical assistance and research facilities in accordance with their interests. The model for this design was Solomon's House. Cowley's Philosophical College, itself conceived after a brief period at Oxford, approached this ideal. We know that in 1657 Wilkins was considering endowing a 'Mathematico-Chymico-Mechanical School', which Evelyn suggested should be modelled on Solomon's House, its members being sworn to secrecy. He himself then elaborated a plan for such a college, a romantic conception, based on the Carthusian monastic organization, in which natural philosophers could pursue their studies apart from the distractions of the world [30]. These were the plans for the future role of science, held by the most influential members of the scientific community, as the Puritan revolution came to an end. The Restoration of Charles II in 1660 provided an unexpected opportunity for the realization of their schemes. The Restoration brought many natural philosophers to London, where, taking advantage of Charles's interest in science, they established the Royal Society.

In some ways this was a satisfactory outcome for science. It achieved an institutional base, with regular periodical publications which became the envy of Europe. Its supporters claimed it to be the fulfilment of Bacon's Solomon's House and the idealization of his philosophy. Comenius dedicated to the Society his *Via Lucis* (1668), a work originally intended to guide the *collegium lucis* at the outset of the Puritan revolution. However, the *collegium lucis* and Royal Society belonged to completely different social and intellectual milieux, with contrasting views on the role of science in education and society. To the utopian reformers of the earlier period, science was a means to realize the physical conditions of the ideal state, by providing man with a sound knowledge of his environment, which could be applied to restore his dominion over nature. It was thus an important foundation subject for education, being necessary for men of all social levels. Science was therefore an important factor in the evolution of a concept of equality of educational provision, since it was an important constituent in the common basic curriculum, which would have involved a much higher level of educational attainment from the lower classes than had previously been thought necessary or possible. In spite of these educational ambitions, the reformers were stigmatized as anti-intellectual enthusiasts by their opponents, a reputation which was incurred by their contempt for the learned professions and universities. Their censures of established institutions provoked suspicions which quenched parliamentary sympathy for their more constructive proposals. However, as exhibited by the subsequent history of education during the Restoration, their ideas on curricular reform were realized in the nonconformist academies which in many ways were the lineal descendants of Dury's 'Reformed School'.

These enlightened academies served only an élite of the dissenters. The majority of the population continued to receive the rudimentary education which was thought appropriate to their condition. Upper-class education also continued much as before, experimental natural philosophy and medicine having only a limited role in formal education. Paradoxically, however, there was a growing curiosity about science at the dilettante level, the 'virtuoso' becoming a favourite target for the Restoration satirist.

Through the virtuosi, experimental science was reduced to a level which became an integral part of the aristocratic taste for generations to come. Sprat applauded the 'generous Breeding which has been given to the Experimental Knowledge of this Age and Country'. This breeding poured into the *Philosophical Transactions* and Royal Society meetings, with fragmentary and disconnected observations on natural history. Sprat was anxious to undermine critics by giving assurances that the Society would not prejudice social and religious institutions; 'all the various manners of *Education,* will remain undisturb'd' [31]. Thus the Royal Society, like the Wilkins circle at Oxford in the previous decade, was able to smooth the entry of science into the aristocratic sensibility, divesting it of ideas on social and educational reform which had been an integral concern of the science advocated by Hartlib and his associates. This manoeuvre was successful, giving the Royal Society great prestige, although relegating it to a peripheral social role. Its failure to maintain the earlier initiative for educational reform was particularly significant, resulting in a growing gulf between the educated classes and the advanced science of the Newtonian age. On the one hand, through the limitation of educational opportunity, the nation's reservoir of scientific talent was not exploited; on the other, the conservatism of traditional education produced an élite unacquainted with science. By failing to realize the implications of the dichotomy between educational practice and the most advanced intellectual developments, the Royal Society was perhaps contributing to its own ultimate decline. Its mistake was repeated at a national level. Consequently, England advanced towards the technological age with a population ill-equipped to take the fullest advantage of its resources.

## Notes

[1] Francis Bacon, *Of the Proficience and Advancement of Learning in Two Books* (1605), Bk. I, sect. iv, paras. 2–3.
[2] Bacon, *Novum Organum* (1620), Bk. I, aph. lxxx; see also aph. cvii.
[3] Bacon, *Of the Proficience and Advancement of Learning*, Bk. I, sect. v, para. 11.
[4] J. A. Comenius, *A Reformation of Schooles* (1642), p. 47.
[5] Comenius, *A Pattern of Universall Knowledge* (1651), p. 21.
[6] S. Hartlib, Preface to J. Dury, *The Reformed School* (1650).
[7] W. Dell, *The Tryal of Spirits* (1653), Appendix: 'The Right Reformation of Learning', p. 26.
[8] Comenius, *A Pattern of Universall Knowledge*, pp. 29–30; see also p. 52.
[9] 'Some Proposalls towards the Advancement of Learning', *Hartlib Papers* (Sheffield University Library), Vol. XLVII. This text is given in full in my *Samuel Hartlib and the Advancement of Learning* (Cambridge, 1970). Citations below are to this edition.
[10] Ibid., p. 179.
[11] W. Petty, *The Advice of W.P. to Mr Samuel Hartlib, for the Advancement of Some Particular Parts of Learning* (1648), pp. 3–4.
[12] G. Winstanley, *The Law of Freedom* (1652). See particularly ch. 5.
[13] Ibid., p. 43.
[14] Ibid., p. 56.
[15] Dury, *The Reformed School*, p. 48.
[16] J. Hall, *An Humble Motion to the Parliament of England Concerning the Advancement of Learning* (1649), pp. 33–4.
[17] T. Sprat, *History of the Royal Society* (1667), p. 113.
[18] Petty, op. cit., p. 5.
[19] C. Dymock, *An Essay for Advancement of Husbandry Learning* (1653).
[20] Dury, op. cit., p. 4.
[21] Ibid., p. 21.

[22] B. Gerbier, *To all Fathers of Families and Lovers of Knowledge* (1648).
[23] W. Sprigge, *A Moderate Plea for a Free and Equal Commonwealth* (1659).
[24] A. Cowley, *Proposition for the Advancement of Experimental Philosophy* (1661).
[25] Ibid., Preface.
[26] Hall, op. cit., p. 5.
[27] Ibid., p. 27.
[28] 'The Humble Petition of Severall Members of the University of Oxon.', *Hartlib Papers*, XLVII.
[29] Wilkins and Ward, *Vindiciae Academiarum* (1654), pp. 49–50.
[30] Letter from Evelyn to Boyle, 3 September 1659, Evelyn's *Diary and Correspondence*, ed. W. Bray, 1854 ed., vol. III, pp. 116–20.
[31] Sprat, op. cit., pp. 323–4.

W. H. G. ARMYTAGE

# Augustan academic honeycombs: some eighteenth-century conventicles of science

I

Prevised by Bacon, evangelized by Comenius and epitomized by the Royal Society and the Académie des Sciences, the ecumenism of science was preached and practised throughout the eighteenth century, in some 220 academies that took shape between 1660 and 1790. Whether national (like the Académie des Sciences of Paris) or local (like the Lunar Society of Birmingham), these academies by their meetings, publications and correspondence, constituted an embryo international network, anticipating, say, and rehearsing, perhaps, the S in UNESCO. Like cells in a honeycomb, these two hundred or so academies were repositories for apiarian industry [1].

The image lies at the heart of my observations, for, just as honey is collected from plants by bees, so the science of these academies fed the plantocratic nature of eighteenth-century society. By just how much can be seen from Erasmus Darwin's great science-fiction extravaganza *The Botanic Garden.* Such a title encompassed his euphoric fantasies of steam aeroplanes and diving bells [2].

These men knew what they were about. As early as 1667 a Swedish nobleman, Bengt Skytte (1643–83) suggested the establishment of a city of the wise which he called Sophopolis. This was to be a kind of Baconian 'Solomon's House' equipped for every kind of scientific research. Skytte sent his proposal to the Royal Society, which was, I suppose, doing a similar job anyway. So he secured from the Elector of Brandenburg a site at Tangermünde on the Elbe together with some funds. This prototype of UNESCO was to be equipped with 'libraries, a museum, laboratories, a botanic garden, a printing press with foreign type faces', and other equipment for an international centre of scholars of all religions and races [3].

Though Skytte's project never got down to earth (if that is not too unkind a metaphor for such an apparently visionary scheme), that of Leibnitz did. Consider his argument (not a new one) that universities should emancipate themselves from monkish erudition, which lacked 'experience, activity and reality', and become centres of reconciliation where 'savants and students should participate as much as possible in the conversation and be as much as they can with other people and in the world', This 'entirely new maxim' could best be fostered by a society of erudite Germans issuing a biennial journal containing accounts of current advances in mathematics, medicine, commerce and manufacturers; co-operating with French, Italian and English academies; co-ordinating scientific research, and licensing the publication of books. This proposed society, he later thought, would accelerate the application of chemical and physiological discoveries to life, by including education, history, economics and what we would now call sociology with its scope of operations. Even children and prisoners could, he argued, furnish material for its investigations. So an 'appetite for curiosity' would be cultivated, the academy would become a bank of useful ideas, a centre of report and a promoter of 'trade and commerce in sciences' [4].

For forty-seven years Leibnitz tried to institutionalize this concept. He corresponded with scientists at home and abroad, immersed himself in the technological life of the day, designing calculating machines (which his mechanic Oliver tried to make) and pumps for the Harz mines. He even entered the political field, and tried to stop European war by suggesting that the King of France should 'Europeanize' Egypt.

He appealed to the Leopoldine Academy, the most active of the local scientific groups in Germany at that time, to unite other German groups around them and become a truly imperial society sheltering and sustaining scientific research, surveying, sifting and solving problems affecting life. By doing so, Leibnitz urged, they would do more in ten years than humanity had effected in centuries.

The movement for such an imperial society got under way when Weigel suggested in 1694 that a group of consultants should be convened to reform the calendar. Profits were to subsidize further work in astronomy, mathematics and the arts. When this did become a burning issue in Brandenburg five years later, Leibnitz introduced an ingenious variation that the profits should be used to establish an observatory and a learned society.

So Leibnitz got his way and the Berlin Academy of Sciences took shape under his presidency. It provided for three interest groups: *Res physico-mathematicae, Lingua Germanica* and *Res literarae*. But it took a further ten years before it established itself. Not until 1710 were its first transactions *Miscellanea Berolinensia* published, and then in Latin. Poor Leibnitz, meanwhile, was saddled with the task of writing a history of the House of the Guelphs.

Leibnitz hoped that scientists in each of the capitals of Europe would gather together to help one another. To help them do so he worked on a Universal Language (which he called a 'Universal Characteristic'), for all current knowledge to be read off by those anxious to apply it. The centre of this movement was to be Britain, followed three years later by Dresden and Leipzig (where Tschunkhausen was working on a mathematico-physical society). War cut short his plans, but Leibnitz, undismayed, outlined his plans to the Tsar in 1711 for technological discoveries and expeditions to Siberia. The Tsar in return gave him a pension, and, fourteen years later, an academy was duly founded at St Petersburg which began to do just this [5].

Other major national societies took shape in Madrid (1713), Danzig (1743), Haarlem (1760), Trondhjem (1760), Brussels (1773), Lisbon (1779), Dublin (1782) and Vienna (1783). Earlier I said they knew what they were about. A professor of mathematics at Edinburgh remarked in 1767 that men should be studied in groups, not as individuals. So too in the same year Joseph Priestley urged the formation of such small scientific groups in his *History of Electricity* (1767). And in spite of wars the vision persisted: we find it in St-Simon's project of 1802 for a Council of Newton, an embryonic European technological community, and in 1811, when Coleridge suggested the formation of a Society for Opposing National Antipathies. To supplement it he suggested a British and Foreign Human Society of Science and Literature 'whose Duty', he wrote, 'it would be to watch over, record, and make known Works and Discoveries where ever published, and as soon as published to form a center [sic] of Correspondence for the Man of Genius and Science in all countries'. With such a society, he added 'it would not have been possible for the French to have so successfully and systematically palmed the labors and discoveries of Sweden, Denmark and Germany as their own new lights' [6].

II

These were in what might be called the heart countries of Europe. Let us look at a country on the fringe: Sweden. For it was the Swedish chargé d'affaires at the Court of the German princes who commissioned Leibnitz's pioneer memorandum to the Duke of Württemberg, the embryo of all his later ideas. The first Swede to become a fellow of the Royal Society of London was James Barkman, later Lord Lyonbergh, who signed the Royal Society's membership book in 1667 and used his position to secure the election of fellow countrymen such as Hiärne in 1669 who in turn had helped his fellow countrymen to unlock the geological pantry on which they squatted. Hiärne in 1695 moved into the new quarters of the public chemical laboratory (founded in 1683 as an adjunct to the mining academy in Stockholm) on the island of Kungsholm in Stockholm in such favourable conditions that few experimental scientists in Europe could match. Here his best student was J.G. Gmelin, father of the famous family of German chemists. Then there was Anders Celsius, builder and director of the Uppsala Observatory, who advocated the adoption of the Gregorian Calendar and of the centigrade thermometer, which was called by his name. One thinks also of Samuel Klingenstierna, who in 1755 enabled the famous English instrument maker, John Dollond, to make achromatic compound lenses for telescopes, and won the prize given by the Russian Academy of Sciences (founded in 1725): a fine example of the way in which Sweden could face both ways in science. Sweden had its *Acta* of the Uppsala Academy issued in Latin from 1720 onwards, and its *Handlingar* of the Stockholm Academy of Sciences issued in Swedish from 1741. The Royal Swedish Academy of Sciences, on the other hand, had been founded in 1739 by, amongst others, a Swede who had served for a time as overseer of a coal mine at Newcastle-upon-Tyne: Martin Triewald (1691–1747): an improver of the steam engine. One of the editors of its treatises, Pehr Wargentin, by increasing the sales price of the almanacs which were its basic source of income, virtually put it on its feet. Wargentin's correspondence with scientists in England, Germany, Russia, France and Italy, survives in some 4,000 letters at the academy today, whilst his statistical work on mortality tables unveils the first British efforts in this field by Richard Price in 1783. Another fellow member of the Royal Society of London was Carl Wilhelm Scheele whose chemical observations were translated into English in 1780 by a tutor at the Warrington non-conformist academy, who was then teaching at Halle in Germany. Scheele's *Chemical and Physical Essays* were translated into English by Edmund Cutler four years later, significantly with footnotes written by the lecturer in chemistry at Oxford, Thomas Beddoes.

Beyond the confines of the scientific coterie of the metropolis, William Withering, the eminent Midland doctor and member of the Lunar Society of Birmingham, published his *Scheele's Outlines of*

*Metallurgy* in 1783. Withering's interest in this indicates that one of the most active centres for the diaspora of Swedish science was Birmingham, where he practised medicine. Birmingham was also a centre of steam-engine manufacture, and here Matthew Boulton also arranged for a translation of the work of another Swedish chemist, T.O. Bergman, and fitted up a chemistry laboratory in 1781.

As a doctor, Withering had a professional interest in botany. Indeed he is credited with the discovery of digitalis in the foxglove: useful as a pharmaceutic in cardiac complaints. Since Swedish scientists were equally informative in this field, Withering engaged a friend to translate the *Systema Vegetabilium* of Linnaeus.

Linnaeus helped the British to understand their own pantry — the plantations — and it is no accident that Sir Joseph Banks who founded Kew Gardens employed a Swede as his librarian. This Swede, Daniel Solander, F.R.S., accompanied him on the Endeavour in 1768 and remained in his employ till 1782 when he died and was succeeded by another Swede, Jonas Dryander. Dryander came from Sweden in 1777 and served Banks until he too followed Solander to the grave in 1810. Thanks to them, Soho Square became one of the centres of intellectual resort of late eighteenth-century England.

One of Banks's guests who came in 1783 was the son of a rich Norwich silk merchant. Banks had just received a letter offering him the Herborium, Library and manuscripts of Linnaeus, at a price lower than that at which he had tried and failed to purchase the Herborium of Linnaeus. Banks showed the letter to the young man from Norwich, who promptly bought it and founded the Linnaean Society.

The indispensable tool of mineral and chemical analysis was the blow pipe: a simple but basic interrogatory tool of early modern science. Though used by Swedish chemists, its value was brought home to the English metallurgists by the publication in 1770 of *An Essay towards a System of Minerology by Axel Frederic Cronstedt...to which is added a Treatise on the Pocket-Laboratory, containing An Easy Method, used by the Author, for trying Mineral Bodies.* Cronstedt's own exploitation of it had already revealed the existence of a metal which he called nickel (a short version of *Kupfernickel* or devil's copper). Amongst the English improvers of the blowpipe was E.D. Clarke. To him Swedish mineral deposits and the way they were analysed were so important that he organized a party of Cambridge men to go there in 1799. It included T.R. Malthus (who had just written the first draft of his essay on population) and William Otter (whose name was to survive in the college bearing his name at Chichester) [7].

## III

The case history of Sweden could be followed by others centred round France and Germany. But I used it to illustrate just how important was the supportive role of the local academies and societies in this international network. For the Lunar Society of Birmingham was but one of many such groups in France and Germany. France had some forty-five or so, formed between 1660 and 1776: Soissons (1674), Nîmes (1682), Angers (1685), Villefranche en Beaujolais (1679), Toulouse (1684), Lyons (1700, 1724 and 1778), Caen (1705), the Société Royale des Sciences of Montpellier (1706), Bordeaux (1712), Rouen (1716, 1735, 1744), Périgueux (1718), Pau (1720), Béziers (1723), Marseilles (1726), Toulouse (1729), Montauban (1730), La Rochelle (1732), Arras (1738, 1778), Dijon (1740), Clermont (1747), Auxerre (1749), Amiens, Nancy, Châlons-sur-Marne (1750), Millau (1751), Besançon (1752), Bourg (1755), Metz (1757), Lille (1758), Grenoble (1772), Mulhouse (1775), and Agen (1776) [8].

Above them all was the Académie des Sciences, which had been reorganized in 1699, given a formal constitution and a remarkably talented secretary, and required to meet every Wednesday and Saturday, with five public assemblies a year. Attendance was made compulsory (the threat of expulsion hung over any absentee). A hierarchy of grades was set up: ten honoraries, twenty pensioners, twenty associates and twenty assistants – a nomenclature not unfamiliar in the university world today. Its *Histoire et Mémoires* comprised an annual report of the papers read at its meetings [9].

The talented secretary was B. de Fontenelle, an able synthesizer of new knowledge; the weather man for the liberal climate of opinion that made eighteenth-century France the Mecca of the cultural world. His forty-four-year tenure of office made him such a venerable figure that Voltaire depicted him as the secretary of the 'Academy of Saturnia' in his *Micromégas* [10]. Fontenelle believed an élite should lead the thought of a nation. This élite needed knowledge, and to provide it an exhaustive inquiry into all manufacturing processes was instituted. This inquiry was entrusted to René Antoine Ferchault de Réaumur and it lasted for both their lives. Published in a continuous series of 121 parts during the years 1761 to 1789 this survey of arts and crafts marks the emergence of modern technology [11].

A similar passion for visiting, reporting and criticizing workshops, factories and industrial centres also animated D. Diderot to undertake another great French publication – the twenty-eight-volume Encyclopedia which was issued between the years 1751 and 1772. Between old Réaumur and young Diderot little love was lost. Réaumur accused

Diderot of copying from his work, sneered at his lowly origins, and castigated his use of science for political reasons [12].

Réaumur was not the only one who criticized the political slant which Diderot gave to his articles. Even the publishers thought it provident to excise certain passages. The considerable body of critical matter that survived excision was certainly well circulated throughout the provincial academies and may well have contributed to the revolution.

Though France and Britain were at war for an aggregate of sixty years during this period, scientists in those two countries never ceased to communicate with each other [13]. J.T. Desaguliers translated works by French engineers like Marriotte in 1718 and Vaucanson in 1742, and was himself awarded a prize by the Academy of Sciences at Bordeaux. The secretary of the Society of Agriculture, Sciences and Arts at Aix, Jacques Gibelin (1744–1828), translated Kirwan's *Minerology*, Franklin's autobiography and the works of Joseph Priestley. Masonic enthusiasm for diffusing knowledge of the useful sciences and the beaux-arts also linked them together. Thus the Chevalier Ramsay, impressed by the Club de l'Entresol (formed in 1724 by Bolingbroke in the Place Vendôme), fostered Freemasonry in France. One French Mason in England, Helvétius, on returning to France, founded the lodge 'Les Sciences' with La Lande, which embraced all scientist Masons in Paris at that time. He wanted to expand the lodge, but died before he could do. Fortunately La Lande was able to help organize the Grand Orient de France, and this gave birth to the famous Nine Sisters Lodge on 5 July 1776. Les Neuf Soeurs, as it was called, was composed of exceptional people who had published work in the sciences or the arts, or patronized such publication. It was divided into nine sections, each under a commissioner, who was to subsidize further publications. Within two years it had 180 members and an annual intake of twenty a year. Apart from its ritualistic activities it provided lectures on various subjects. When Benjamin Franklin became its master he took a lead in establishing the Société Apollonienne or Musée de Paris for the publication of books and production of lectures. Benjamin Franklin was also a member of more than twenty other societies in 1785, whilst the Berlin Academy of the same year included five Germans, five Swiss, four Huguenots, three French and one Italian [14].

## IV

Let us look at the Berlin scene for a moment, for the Berlin Academy was an embryo scientific civil service. Though neither of its first fellows nor its endowment was up to Leibnitz's expections, it excited the admiration of the English translator of its ordinances and statutes who admired its 'two firm and unshaken pillars, I mean most ample Salarys for the Teachers, and most easy Expenses for the Learners', and exclaimed, 'What a mighty increase of Trade and Wealth will this Institution bring to the City of Berlin?'

Leibnitz was its pillar, writing twelve of the sixty articles in the first volume of its *Miscellanea Berolinensia ad Incrementum Scientiarum*, published in 1710, and these in all three of the subject groups. Talent was bought for it. Like the manager of a modern football team, Frederick the Great coaxed foreign talent to Berlin. He lured Leonard Euler from the St Petersburg Academy in 1744 and when Euler left twenty-two years later, he invited Lagrange who stayed for twenty-one years (from 1766 to 1787), swelling the proceedings of the Academy with his papers and writing his *Mécanique Analytique*. In 1787 Lagrange returned to Paris.

Other members included J.P. Sussmilch, an army chaplain who advocated the application of statistical methods in estimating the industrial and scientific wealth of a nation in a book curiously entitled *The Divine Order* (1742). The Secretary of the Academy, J.H.S. Formey, wrote a counterblast to Rousseau's *Émile*. Life might be quantitative in eighteenth-century Berlin, but it was also quarrelsome.

The real role of the Berlin Academy was to make up for the shortcomings of the barren north-German plains. Having no colonies, the laboratory of the Berlin Academy under Andreas S. Margraf (1709–82) recovered sugar from beetroot in 1746 and showed that a constituent of alum, alumina, is contained in clay. Margraf also ran a class in experimental philosophy.

Other academies were founded at Erfurt in 1753 for the 'Useful Sciences', at Leipzig (in 1768) and in Munich (in 1759). At Dresden a *collegium-medicio-chirurgicum* had been founded in 1748. The great systematizer Albrecht von Haller (1708–77) founded the Königliche Gesellschaft der Wissenschaften in 1751. Author of 13,000 scientific papers, Haller was a learned society in himself—being a physiologist, poet, botanist and novelist. With his *Elementa Physiologiae Corporis Humani* (1757–66) we reach modernity. At Göttingen, too, J.F. Blumenbach (1752–1840) did seminal work in medical ethnology. Shape of skull, facial configuration and colour of the skin he established as criteria in classifying human types. He introduced the category 'Caucasian' to describe the white race because a female Georgian skull was the most symmetric [15].

A veritable ground swell of enthusiasm for technical training flowed in Germany. Johann Georg Leib's *Probe, wie eine Verbesserung Land und Leuten* (1705) had urged the establishment of an academy to improve manufactures whilst at Halle a pupil of Weigel's, Jean Christopher Semler, had put forward a plan for a 'mechanical school'. With A.H. Francke a move was made to introduce the principle into the schools of Halle where he was an inspector. But he found little support and the scheme was abandoned in 1709 and not revived until thirty years later. At Erlangen J.G. Cross and at Leipzig G.H. Zincke were also active promoters of similar ideas.

Frederick the Great utilized this ground swell to encourage the foundation of an Economical-Mathematical Realschul in Berlin where J.J. Hecker was to help pupils 'to apply under various circumstances what they had learned of science and mathematics in the school'. Inspired by the survey of arts and crafts by the French Académie des Sciences, J.G. Busch opened an academy at Hamburg in 1767, concentrating on the commercial aspects of technology. Here Frau von Stein, Goethe's friend, and Alexander von Humboldt were pupils and from here F. Ch. Wurms went to open a similar institution in Wilhelmsdale in 1785. Maria Theresa opened another on his plan, in Vienna in 1770.

Farther south, at Freiberg in Saxony, where the mines had been attracting students like the famous Russian Lomonosov as early as 1739, a mining school had been growing up. Now, in 1766 it was officially recognized. A.G. Werner (1749–1817) was later appointed to its staff. Dogmatic and stimulating, he attracted students by avoiding speculation and stressed the importance of observing facts. From these facts he formed the idea that the sea had the decisive role in the formation of rocks: 'Neptunism' his successors called it.

To Werner's 'Neptunist' school at Freiberg came Russian, Scandinavian, Spanish, Polish, Portuguese and Neapolitan students. Britain was represented by the son of James Watt. Many of these students returned to their own countries to found similar institutions. Andrei Deriabin became director of a Russian mining institute in 1773. Fausto El Huyar set up one in Spain in 1782 and Mexico in 1792. Prussia followed suit with a mining school at Clausthal in 1775 and France established the École des Mines in 1781, where under B.G. Sage, scholarships were provided for sons of miners and peasants who had reached the age of sixteen.

This movement was given a name: 'technology'. The word, significantly enough, was coined by Johann Beckmann (1739–1811), a former student of theology, who turned to mathematics and the natural sciences, visiting the Netherlands, Russia, Sweden and Denmark. Impressed by what he had seen, he initiated lectures on agriculture, mineralogy, market research and financial administration at Göttingen University under the generic title of 'technology'. He wrote a textbook on the subject in 1777 which had run to six editions by 1809. Beckmann also developed into a historian of inventions, and his book on this subject was still being issued in England as late as 1846 [16].

V

Abraham de Moivre, a French exile in England and a private tutor, published his *Doctrine of Chances* in 1716. At the Rainbow Coffee House in 1735 a Society for the Encouragement of Learning 'was established with the general aim of promoting the Arts and Sciences'.

In England, several of such societies were either formed in, or run from, coffee-houses [17]. The first of a long line of English encyclopedias, the *Lexicon Technicum, or a Universal English Dictionary of the Arts and Sciences,* was published in 1704 by John Harris, F.R.S., who taught mathematics at the Marine Coffee House in Birchin Lane. Johann Jacob Dillen or Dillenius (1681–1747), the Sherardian Professor of Botany at Oxford, and John Martyn (1699–1768), an amateur entomologist, formed a Botanical Society in 1721 which also met at the Rainbow Coffee House, in Watling Street, but later changed to a private house and subsequently ceased to exist. An Aurelian Society similarly took shape in the Swan Tavern in the Cornhill, in 1745, till a fire, three years later, destroyed it. In its resurrected form it used to meet at the York Coffee House, in St James Street, and from this was formed the Linnaean Society in 1788.

The President of the Royal Society in 1741, Martin Folkes (1690–1754), was such a habitué of Rawthmell's in Henrietta Street, Covent Garden, that, according to one Fellow, he chose the council and officers out of 'his junto of Sycophants' that used to meet him there every night. Rawthmell's incubated an ambitious venture some thirteen years later: on 22 March 1754, a group of Fellows of the Royal Society listened to the proposals of a Northampton drawing-master to subsidize inventions by prizes, in much the same way as horse-breeding was fostered by competition at the Northampton horse fair. This drawing-master, Shipley, was anxious to find substitutes for cobalt and madder, both dyes used in the cloth trade, both imported, and both difficult to obtain. Meeting again at Rawthmell's on 29 March, they decided to make their meetings more formal, and arranged to forgather regularly at a circulating library in Crane Court, Fleet Street. From this grew the Society for the Encouragement of Arts, Manufactures, and Commerce, better known today as the Royal Society of Arts.

Just as these coffee-houses incubated societies, encyclopedias, newsletters, insurance companies and town libraries, so they provided also a forum and clearing-house for new discoveries in science. At 'Buttons', in Russell Street, Covent Garden, of which Martin Folkes was a member, there was a post-box where intelligence of all kinds was deposited for Addison's paper, the *Guardian*. Fashioned like a lion's head, it stood on the western side of the coffee-house, 'holding its paws under the chin, on a box which contains everything that he swallows'. As Addison remarked, it was 'a proper emblem of knowledge and actions, being all head and paws'. This 'lion post-box' was later moved to the 'Bedford'. This was even more directly concerned with science. There John Stirling, F.R.S., and later J.T. Desaguliers, F.R.S. (1683–1744), lectured on experimental philosophy. Stirling was a friend of Nicholas Bernouilli and Isaac Newton, and later went on to become a mine manager in Lanarkshire. Desaguliers, whom we have met earlier as a translator of French scientific works and a prizeman of a French scientific society, was once a demonstrator at the Royal Society, and discoursed at large over the great piazza at Covent Garden to, amongst others, the Fieldings, Hogarth, Woodward, Lloyd and Goldsmith.

The quacks and bone-setters who frequented these places often picked up more than odd clients. Thus Joshua Ward (1685–1761), so aptly caught by Hogarth in the 'Harlot's Progress', made such good use of the scraps of gossip and information he picked up that in 1736 he was able to manufacture sulphuric acid at Twickenham by the bell process. He reduced the price of this valuable commodity some sixteen-fold. The local inhabitants were so offended by the smell of burning brimstone and nitre that they forced him to remove his distillery to Richmond. By 1749 he had patented his process, and by 1758, when the French metallurgist and 'industrial spy' Gabriel Jars began visiting England, he noticed that Ward was employing Welsh women, probably so that the secret of his work would not be divulged.

A more respectable chemist, Dr Morris had an 'elaboratory' at Robert's Coffee House in the Great Piazza, Covent Garden, where a number of crucibles were tested in 1757. By 1782, a Chemical Society was meeting at the Chapter Coffee House in London [18].

## VI

Of these societies in Europe 70 were founded between 1750 and 1800, 9 in the fifth decade, 6 in the sixth, 6 in the seventh, 20 in the eighth and 29 in the ninth. The first specialist physics journal, Rozier's *Observations sur la Physique,* appeared in 1771, the first chemical journal — Crell's *Chemisches Journal* — in 1778, the first *Botanical Magazine* in 1787. And, next in importance to the *Philosophical Transactions* was *The Philosophical Magazine* (in 1798) [19].

These subject specialist journals were, in time, to replace the *Acta* and *Miscellanea* as reporters on the knowledge industry, reflecting the displacement of the generalist groups of the seventeenth and eighteenth centuries by the specialist societies of the nineteenth century [20]. Yet the displacement only widened the Leibnitzian and Voltairian ideal of an open aristocracy of enlightened service, an ideal further burnished by St-Simon, Comte and H.G. Wells. In Wells's hand it became an 'open' conspiracy of men of science unifying the world. Indeed in optimism, energy and shrewdness he was the last of the eighteenth-century bees: a generalist in an age of specialists who died a disappointed man because he had never been elected a Fellow of the Royal Society [21].

Our own age of negentropy has posed the need for an ever more efficient communications network [22]. This at one level involves yet more invisible colleges (since informal colloquia of top scientists continue to grow outside formal associations). As they rush to their assignments by plane or communicate by transatlantic telephone they play out, in faster tempo, the role more slowly rehearsed by their Augustan forebears, just as the present-day students, in their desire to 'participate' in the discussions on curricula and organization of colleges and universities, are unconscious subscribers to Leibnitz's vision of a university where 'savants and students should participate as much as possible in the conversation and be as much as they can with other people and in the world' [23]. Indeed if we accept his proposition in the *Monadology* (para. 22) that 'every state is a national consequence of its preceding state in such a manner that the present state of it is big with the future', one can identify in the correspondence of himself and his eighteenth-century successors embryonic schemes for ecumenism [24], and educational method [25]. The European technological community of Mr Wilson has very old roots. So has Dewey's ideal of a science-based democracy [26].

# Notes

[1] Nicholas Hans, 'The Rosicrucians of the Seventeenth Century', *Adult Education*, Vol. VII (1935), p.229; F.E. Held, *Christianopolis* (London, 1916), p.203; Martha Ornstein, *The Role of Scientific Societies in the Seventeenth Century* (Chicago, 1928), p.168. Harcourt Brown, *Scientific Organisations in Seventeenth-Century France (1620–80)* (Baltimore, 1934).

[2] Desmond King-Hele, *Erasmus Darwin* (London: Macmillan, 1963).

[3] *Festschrift zu Gustav Schmollers 70. Geburtstag* (Leipzig, 1908), pp.65–99.

[4] R.W. Meyer (trans. J.P. Stern), *Leibnitz and the 17th-Century Revolution* (Cambridge, 1952), p.97.

[5] Ruth Lydia Saw, *Leibnitz* (Penguin Books, 1945); Ernst Cassirer (trans. F.C.A. Koelln and J.P. Pettegrove), *The Philosophy of the Enlightenment* (Princeton, 1951); A. Harnack, *Geschichte der Königlich Preussichen Academie der Wissenschaften zu Berlin* (Berlin, 1900).

[6] Kathleen Coburn, *Inquiring Spirit. A New Presentation of Coleridge from his published and unpublished prose* (London: Routledge & Kegan Paul, 1951), pp.343–4.

[7] W.H.G. Armytage, *Looking North: Influence and Inference from Sweden in English Education* (Peterborough, 1969), pp.4–5; S. Lindroth, *Swedish Men of Science 1650–1950* (Uppsala, 1952).

[8] Bernard Fäy, 'Learned Societies in Europe and America in the Eighteenth Century', *American Historical Review* Vol., XXXVII (1931–2).

[9] B.T. Morgan, *Histoire du Journal des Sçavans, 1665–1700* (Paris, 1929).

[10] Leonard M. Marsak, 'Fontenelle in defence of Science', *Journal of the History of Ideas*, Vol. XX (1959), pp.111–22.

[11] F. Klemm, *A History of Western Technology* (London: Allen & Unwin, 1959).

[12] Douglas H. Gordon and N.L. Torrey, *The Censoring of Diderot's Encyclopédie and the Re-established Text* (New York: Columbia University Press, 1947); Jean Thomas, *L'Humanisme de Diderot* (Paris: Société d'édition 'Les Belles lettres', 1932); Joseph Le Gras, *Diderot et l'Encyclopédie* (Amiens: E. Malfère, 1928); Arthur M. Wilson, *Diderot, the Testing Years 1713–1759* (New York: Oxford University Press, 1957).

[13] Gavin de Beer, *The Sciences were never at War* (London, 1960), IX, who gives many case-histories.

[14] Louis Amiable, *Une Loge Masonnique, La Proix Les Neuf Soeurs* (Paris, 1897); N. Hans, 'UNESCO of the Eighteenth Century: La Loge des Neuf Soeurs and its venerable master, Benjamin Franklin', *Am. Phil. Society,* Vol. XCVII, pp.513–24.

[15] Erik Amburger, *Die Mitglieder der Deutschen Akademie der Wissenschaften zu Berlin 1700–1950* (Berlin, 1950), p.12; J.G. Hagen, *Index Operum Leonardi Euler* (Berlin, 1896).

[16] W.H.G. Armytage, *The Rise of the Technocrats* (London, 1969).

[17] Bryant Lillywhite, *London Coffee Houses. A Reference Book of Coffee Houses of the Seventeenth, Eighteenth and Nineteenth Centuries* (London: George Allen & Unwin, 1963).

[18] E.F. Robinson, *The Early History of Coffee Houses in England* (London: Kegan Paul, 1893); Aytoun Ellis, *The Penny Universities: A History of the Coffee Houses* (London: Secker & Warburg, 1956); M. 'Espinasse, *Robert Hooke* (London: William Heinemann, 1956); A.T. Gage, *A History of the Linnean Society of London* (London: The Linnaean Society, 1938); Karl Mannheim, *Essays on the Sociology of Culture* (London: Routledge & Kegan Paul, 1956).

[19] D.A. Kronick, *History of Scientific Periodicals* (New York, 1962).

[20] G. Millerson, *The Qualifying Associations; A Study in Professionalisation* (London: Routledge & Kegan Paul, 1964).

[21] Albert Guérard, 'The New History: H.G. Wells and Voltaire', *Scribner's Magazine,* No. 76 (1924), pp.476–84.

[22] Alvin M. Weinberg, 'The Third international Conference on Science and Society', *Bulletin of the Atomic Scientists,* Vol. XXV (November 1969), pp.23–6.

[23] Meyer, op. cit., p.97.

[24] G.J. Jordan, *The Reunion of the Churches: A Study of G.W. Leibnitz and his great attempt* (London, 1927).

[25] John Davidson, *A new interpretation of Herbart's psychology and educational theory through the philosophy of Leibniz* (Edinburgh, London, 1906).

[26] One of Dewey's first books was actually on Leibnitz – in 1888.

H. C. MORGAN

# The curriculum of training in the fine arts in the nineteenth century

The curriculum of fine arts training which will be examined is that found in two sorts of establishment during the period. The one is, in modern parlance, the privately owned sector of art education, namely, the Royal Academy. The other is the great state-directed area of art training comprising those establishments which at the end of the nineteenth century were under the Department of Science and Art. Within these two are found all the essential ideas relevant to art training and curriculum. By 'fine arts' I refer to the more restricted sense of the words, i.e. those arts appertaining to design in painting, sculpture and architecture, and, since art curriculum comes out of contemporaneous art thinking, it will be necessary at times to say something of this background.

The Royal Academy of Arts in London was by no means the first of its kind, not even in England [1]. Its significance lay in its mode of foundation. It was a *royal* academy, founded personally by George III who throughout his long life was greatly attached to it. It had influence, and it acquired wealth and great weight. Moreover, it had as its first President a remarkable man, Sir Joshua Reynolds, whose ideas — as will be seen — ran not merely behind the art training offered in the Royal Academy Schools but also, in considerable measure, through that of the state-directed system of the nineteenth century. Without more ado then, and conscious that I leave many very interesting things unsaid [2], I turn to Reynolds and his Academy.

After Reynolds returned to England from Italy in 1753 he rapidly established for himself a high reputation as a fashionable London portrait painter. His paintings immediately began to reflect his Italian studies — in compositional arrangements, figure handling, use of drapery and background, in colour treatment — in short, in the qualities of imagination [3]. He was applying to the near-trade of portraiture [4] the tenets of the Grand Style, or History Painting, or High

Art. These were the most commonly-used terms describing the art of the Italian High Renaissance. He was also the intimate friend of many influential persons of his time, and was in every way the ideal person to be first President. Once established, he set himself the task of delivering annually in the Royal Academy a Discourse to the students and guests, on the occasion of prize-giving. There are fifteen Discourses in all, written between 1769 and 1790 [5]. Reynolds worked very hard at these, and they are to this day highly regarded. Many were translated into Italian, French and German during his lifetime, and more than thirty English editions have appeared since his death. The Discourses had a great and immediate effect on the curriculum and training offered in the Royal Academy Schools, which Schools were the sole institution of any weight offering art instruction in England from 1768 to 1837. Subsequently they affected other created institutions. What then are the essentials of the Discourses?

The Discourses urged that the artist must, above all, be equipped scholastically. Reynolds shows how painters, sculptors and architects of all periods achieved much to be noted, and that the roots of high art are found also in great literature, history, drama, and the Bible. The painting of history, in the fullest sense of the term, ought, he says, to be the goal of the finest artists. He advocated hard work and disciplined thinking, and exhorted youth to pursue these, there being no 'shorter path to excellence' [6]. Rules have their place [7]. Rules, he believed, are only to be discarded when a stage of excellence is reached. Rules, he says, are not fetters to genius, 'they are only fetters to men of no genius' [8]. He places great value on the representation of Ideal Beauty, a desideratum of ennobling art. Beauty may 'conclude in Virtue' [9], and his concept of it is akin to religion. But since Ideal Beauty is a 'sight never beheld...nor has the hand expressed it' [10], the artist must attempt it by the eclectic mode of study of classical Greece [11]. He must select aspects of the better forms of nature, and use the best in the highest art. And, logically, there must be a hierarchical evaluation of art forms and national schools [12]. Of these the highest were the schools of the Italian High Renaissance, and the lowest were the genre, landscape and still-life painting of the Dutch [13]. To the young painter or sculptor Reynolds offered the highest aims. The artist was to ennoble, he should be a seer-poet, one of the élite, and one whose works and existence might enrich his nation [14] and serve his God.

The thinking of the Discourses carried into the practice of the Royal Academy Schools in, for example, their mode of teaching by rules. The probationer-student began in the Antique Academy, and there he learnt to draw from casts of antique statuary, under the keeper or principal of that department of the Schools. From thence he proceeded, after successful examination, into the Life School where he spent a great deal of time drawing (not painting [15]) from the life. There was also regular instruction in perspective and anatomy. And there was much hard work, suitably rewarded by numerous medals and premiums. Some idea of the drudgery of the early training may be obtained from Frith's account of his experiences in Sass's drawing school, which was a sort of preparatory school for the Royal Academy Schools. The practice in such a school was similar to that to be met with in the Academy, so Frith's account is not misplaced:

> The master had prepared with his own hand a great number of outlines from the antique, beginning with Juno's eye and ending with the Apollo — hands, feet, mouths, faces, in various positions, all in severely correct outline. The young student, beginning with Juno's eye, was compelled to copy outlines that seemed numberless; some ordered to be repeated again and again, till Mr Sass could be induced to place the long-desired 'Bene' at the bottom of them. This course, called 'drawing from the flat', was persisted in till the pupil was considered advanced enough to be allowed to study the mysteries of light and shade. A huge white plaster ball, standing on a pedestal, was the next object of attention; by the representation of which in Italian chalk and on white paper the student was to be initiated into the first principles of light, shadow and rotundity. ...I spent six weeks over that awful ball (the drawing exists still, a wonder of line-work), the result being a certain amount of modelling knowledge very painfully acquired. Then came a gigantic bunch of plaster grapes, intended to teach differences of tone (I soon learnt what tone meant) in a collection of objects, with the lights and shadows and reflections peculiar to each. How I hated and despised this second and, I thought, most unnecessary trial of my patience! but it was to be done, and I did it. Then permission was given for an attempt at a fragment from the antique in the form of a hand. Thus step by step I advanced, till I was permitted to draw from the entire figure. ...I could feel no interest in what I was about. Perspective bewildered me, 'and to this day I know little or nothing about that dreadful science; and anatomy and I parted after a very short and early acquaintance. [16]

So much for the student impressions of one of the most popular of Victorian painters, and one whose works were three times protected by a rail in the Royal Academy exhibitions, so that the press of the crowds should not damage them.

The pursuit of the ideal and the practice of eclecticism were constantly before the students. Sir Anthony Carlisle, dressed in full court dress with bag-wig and cocked hat was a great exhibitionist and illustrator of the theme in his lectures on anatomy. On one occasion he used a troupe of Chinese jugglers, and in 1821 he exceeded his own spectacularism by arranging a squad of nude Life-Guardsmen to show how the muscles were exercised when using the broadsword. So numerous was the crowd that the doors had to be shut and guarded by Bow Street constables, but many of the disappointed mob clambered over the roof to peer in through the skylights [17]. So great was the confusion that proceedings had to be brought to a close by the President. Another illustration of teaching to the ideal by way of naturalism concerns a cast which hangs to this day in the Royal Academy Schools. It is of a crucified man, and its history is most interesting. Various Academicians — West, Cosway and the sculptor Banks — had become interested in artists' representations of the crucified Christ. In this the practice had been, for centuries, to use either a living model suspended by ropes, or a corpse. It was clear that neither could give the true effect, and these artists believed that a nearer approximation might be obtained to a dying figure if they attached to a cross a body from which the warmth of life had not yet departed. So they approached the eminent surgeon Carpue, who obtained permission from the Surgeon-General to the Forces to use the body of a Chelsea pensioner who was to be hanged for the murder of a comrade. After the hanging the corpse was immediately attached to a cross, and an extremely delicate and skilful casting was made from the excoriated body by Banks [18]. Macabre? Perhaps, but it is illustrative of the thoroughness of the pursuit of artistic knowledge which was a feature of the time.

Hierarchical evaluation also took root. Haydon wrote, of the Antique School Keeper [19]: 'I told him I would never paint portraits — but devote myself to High Art. "Keep to dat!" said Fuseli, looking fiercely at me. "I will, Sir." ' Haydon tried to, but he had not even the small salary stipulated by Samuel Palmer, who maintained that 'a person living as an epic poet should be able to exist on 5s. 2d. per week' [20]. In the event, young artists took what they might of the idealism, depending on their talents and abilities, and did what they could to earn a living. Many drifted into whatever field offered money — portraiture, subject-painting, book-illustration and industrial design. Architects and sculptors could usually find work, even if this was at a humbler level than high art.

It is time now to turn from training in the Royal Academy Schools. It carried on thus, with minor changes and modifications, right through the nineteenth century. So much so that even the very loyal Academician G.D. Leslie, son of an equally loyal Academician father, felt compelled to write, in 1902: 'The teaching in our Schools has in point of fact been running far too long on the same system under which the Schools were founded over a hundred and thirty years ago...' [21]. When Sir George Clausen delivered his lectures in the Royal Academy on Impressionism, between 1906 and 1913, a landmark was reached. At last the seat of traditionalism had begun to note a modern movement — but this was manifestly too late to save the stick-in-the-mud reputation of the establishment which is found to this day. Yet, if the Royal Academy system of art training in the late nineteenth century seemed rigorous and traditional, one has also to admit that the system organized by the Department of Science and Art was manifestly duller, for its weight of non-creative work was even more exacting. It is to that system that I now turn. To do so it is necessary to go back to Haydon.

For much of the first half of the nineteenth century the tempestuous, ardent and talented Benjamin Robert Haydon was a powerful force in art thinking, and he was constantly before the notice of the public. He had two strong convictions. One was that high art alone was worthy of attention: the other, that the Royal Academy was a pernicious establishment which had traduced its high calling to foster and encourage that high art. Also he believed, not without cause, that it had done him personally much harm. So, with the bitterness of personal conviction he attacked it throughout the years. In the 1820s he began to look elsewhere for active support in the cause of history painting, and in 1823 he memorialized Parliament, this being the first of a series of such petitions. When, several years later, he was commissioned to paint the Reform Banquet — even Haydon had to paint some portraits! — he made the most of his opportunities to put across his ideas to the Radical leaders. In his own words [22]: '...a couple of eyes were dashed in as I proved to their lord-ships no minister thought at all on the subject! and I often finished a noble lord's mouth, as I demolished his arguments against a vote of public money.' Others, too, from a far less elevated viewpoint than Haydon, were concerned with the inadequacy of art education in England, for there had been a considerable decline in the sale of British products and manufactures — textiles, metalwork, furniture, pottery and fancy goods wherein good aesthetic standards ought to have been evident. When Haydon said that the art education in England was at fault, and that the Royal Academy Schools were to blame for this, there were powerful industrialists and members of parliament who were prepared to go along with him. They knew the end products were not good, and they were prepared to accept his explanation that that fault lay in the schooling of the Royal Academy, a schooling which, at that time, was a monopoly. As a result, a Parliamentary Select Committee was set up in 1835, accepting the terms of Ewart:

> to enquire into the best means of extending a knowledge of the arts and principles of design among the people (especially the manufacturing population) of the country; also to enquire into the constitution of the Royal Academy and the effects of institutions connected with the Arts.

By the time the report was printed the specific reference to the Royal Academy was omitted, the wording of the second part being:

> ...to enquire into the Constitution, Management and Effects of Institutions connected with the Arts.

But, whatever the wording, the effect was the same — the Royal Academy and its Schools were under heavy fire. (Another reason, incidentally, why that establishment was so constantly attacked by the Radicals was that at that time it shared the present National Gallery building with the National Collection, and so, in the opinion of many, it was unduly privileged.) The fascinating story of that Select Committee must be ignored here. It dragged on until the next year, but even before the second session began the Board of Trade requested £1,600 of the Treasury to set up a Normal School of Design in July 1836. This was the start of the whole state-directed system of art education in the nineteenth century. From this developed many provincial schools of design which later became municipal art colleges. From the London School, initially established at Somerset House, came the developments at South Kensington which ultimately became the Victoria and Albert Museum and the Royal College of Art. Haydon had indeed triumphed. Schools of design were under way.

Before turning to the schools of design, however, it is well to make a very brief diversion and mention the interest in art taken by the Mechanics' Institutes. Yapp, writing in 1853, said of these:

> Our Mechanics' Institutions alone can lay claim to attempt to introduce drawing and modelling to the people. Their means have limited the amount of their usefulness; and, doubtless, many of them, left to their own resources as to the plan to be pursued, have done little more than follow the old school system of copying third-rate drawings, and multiplying trash...thus we find in many institutions that drawing-classes have been established, but have not obtained the support of members. In others, fortunately, the case

has been very different. [23]

There is much that could be said of the Mechanics' Institutes and art education generally. Haydon, after all, found lecturing in them to be most rewarding. But in so far as they had effects on the art training curriculum of the nineteenth century the above quotation summarizes the matter adequately.

I return to the schools of design, an account of which has been written by Professor Quentin Bell. This is lucid, soundly reasoned, witty, and is an excellent short guide to the activities of so many schools over a considerable period of time, and anyone investigating the transactions of the schools of design must look to that account, as I do here. The temptation must be resisted to follow Bell in looking at the conflicts between administrators and artist-teachers, the quarrels of incompatible personalities, the parts played by students, Royal Academicians, and manufacturers, and the ultimate rise to power of Henry Cole. For, when all the disputes had died down, Henry Cole was there in charge, a powerful civil servant and the creator of the system which sprang from the schools of design in 1852. This was the Department of Practical Art, soon to be styled the Department of Science and Art. In the fifteen years' existence of the schools of design, spotlights had played on the quarrels of Dyce and Haydon, Heath Wilson and Herbert, Heath Wilson and his staff, and, ultimately, Henry Cole and Stafford Northcote. But what was all the trouble about? Why did the original schools of design quarrel themselves out of existence?

Bell says, rightly, that the difficulties were, firstly, administrative, secondly, doctrinal. The administrative side has little to do with the content of this paper, fascinating though it is; therefore let us look at the doctrinal aspect.

The doctrine of the schools of design, as established in 1837, was simple. Henry Cole is very clear in his assessment of what this was:

...the express purpose...was to provide for the architect, the upholsterer, the weaver, the printer, the potter, and all manufacturers, artizans better educated to originate and execute their respective wares, and to invest them with greater symmetry of form, with increased harmony of colour, and with greater fitness of decoration; to render manufactures not less useful by ornamenting them, but more beautiful and therefore more useful. [24].

But such simplicity was not to be. Coming right into the arena, almost at once, was the academic doctrine of high art. This, obviously, is not surprising since the Royal Academy Schools had been preaching the doctrine for decades. The struggle then became that of better training for high art versus practical training for ornament and design in manufactures. Dyce, first Director of the London School and distinguished Royal Academician though he was, stood for the latter — a pragmatic, non-academic form of training. And he was at considerable pains to see his ideas and ideals established, not sparing himself in travelling in England and on the Continent, touring factories and studying training systems. Haydon, until his dramatic suicide in 1846, was Dyce's constant antagonist. Haydon, indeed, forced Dyce to allow the study of life drawing in the London School, and thus modified at least Dyce's practice if not his theory. Haydon also stirred up the Manchester School of Design when its council proposed to abolish figure study, and he writes of the students there eagerly awaiting his return as their champion:

> ...this is going on like the early Christians. Persecution like this will make the thing. These councils and pupils here are doing what is being done by councils and pupils in many of the great towns at which I have lectured...in London, the moment my back is turned they seek to undo all the good I have done. [25]

When Heath Wilson was appointed in place of Dyce it was not long before there was open student revolt at Somerset House, the students and Herbert fighting the Director. Herbert, a Royal Academician, stood for liberal study of a more academic nature, and the letter of protest which the students sent to the Board of Trade was, in effect, demanding their right to be trained as artists and not merely as ornamental designers. Yet strange things happened! Heath Wilson survived the storm, and took on to his staff Alfred Stevens, an excellent designer who favoured the Continental approach to art training for industry, the view that traditional training in art came first and expertise in some special branch might follow. Not only did Wilson appoint Stevens but in the fifth report of the School in 1846 he did a volte-face. He proudly claimed that every student had first to pass through a course of human figure drawing as 'promoting refinement of taste', and the whole emphasis of his school was now towards academic art. After Heath Wilson was removed to his new appointment as Director and Inspector of the Provincial Schools, the same ideological struggle continued until Cole decided to take over. Cole had a flair for administration and tremendous powers of determination, resilience and cunning to gain his ends. He made excellent use of the press (his own!) [26] and was instrumental in setting up the Select Committee of 1849 which he more or less controlled through his friend, the chairman Milner Gibson. Cole's successful role in the 1851 Great Exhibition was his trump card, and in 1852 he achieved control of the newly formed Department of Practical Art, as has already been said. It now seemed as if the ideological strife would be ended.

Things are rarely simple, however, or merely black and white. Cole took with him to his new department Richard Redgrave. Redgrave was a Royal Academician, trained in its Schools. Further, though he was Cole's lieutenant and worked with him for more than twenty years, there was always liberality in his outlook. Indeed, the personalities of Cole and Redgrave affected each other. The liberality of Redgrave is seen in his evidence given before the 1863 Royal Commission on the Royal Academy. He was called in as one who knew extremely well the practices of both the schools of design and the Royal Academy Schools. He stated that the South Kensington schools could be considered as a sort of preliminary to the Royal Academy Schools, though, of course, it was not necessary for South Kensington students to proceed there. He instanced this in the training of architects, modellers, and painters. At South Kensington, as in the Royal Academy Schools, certificates were granted in human figure drawing, painting, and other traditional aspects of art training. Of the South Kensington figure certificate he said:

> In drawing from the antique, after the student has made his drawing he is required to analyze it anatomically; his skeleton is placed within the outline, and afterwards the muscles, from the best information he can get, and all the parts of the skeleton and muscles must correspond with the different points of the figure. [27]

This practice was entirely in line with that of the Royal Academy Schools. Design for industry, indeed! How Haydon would have laughed.

Another factor which changed the order of priorities in the head school at South Kensington was a new national educational need, and with this new need came a change in curriculum emphasis. When the Committee of Council in Education decided that art should become part of the curriculum of elementary schools, it looked to the South Kensington school to provide the necessary instruction to schoolmasters. Cole appeared to approve of this. It was a straightforward task, and, moreover, so great was the consequent press upon the school that South Kensington could unquestionably be excused if it devoted a little less attention to art training for manufacturers [28]! The changed system became tight and tidy. South Kensington taught the art teachers, who then taught some promising pupils along the same lines, first in the elementary schools and then in the provincial schools of design. These in turn came to South Kensington to train as art teachers – and so it went on. Country-wide art training became a huge inbred mass of conformity and regulation.

Did the captains of industry object to this redirection at South Kensington, with its side effect of reducing the importance and facilities for industrial art training? Scarcely at all! The pattern throughout, from the inception in 1837, had been an unwillingness on the part of the manufacturers to support the schools of design. There is much evidence in the 1864 Select Committee on Schools of Art to this effect. At Stoke-on-Trent:

> Mr Hollins ...stresses that the manufacturers generally have failed to show their appreciation of the School... and that he does not believe that if the government grant were withdrawn, they would support it themselves. ...The evidence from Halifax, from Paisley, and from Norwich is much to the same effect.... At Lambeth...it would be impossible to get subscriptions ...At Chester, where the school is considered very successful, there are no subscriptions at all. [29]

So the manufacturers were happy, or indifferent. As for Henry Cole, he had seen the possible embarrassment of a strong emphasis on industrial training. Of him, Bell says:

> It must have been bitter for Cole to discover that he could be thwarted as Dyce had been thwarted, that the students still wanted to be artists and that the industrialists still insisted that all technical training should be undertaken in their own workshops. [30]

Both Redgrave and Cole wrote books to support their art training mode. Redgrave wrote an *Elementary Manual of Colour* which was much used by art students, glass-painters and embroiderers. Diagrams of harmonies of primary, secondary and tertiary hues were inserted, and much was made also of contrast and proportion. Cole, under the pseudonym Felix Summerly, wrote for children. One such book, *First Exercises for Children*, gives many exercises in copying lines and shapes, and the text takes the form of simple question and answer, ranging widely over the elementary field. Both men led very active lives, and were constantly being called upon to carry out some office in the world of art. Both travelled around England in the course of their duties, and both were frequently asked to travel widely over Europe in search of items for the South Kensington museum and collection. Redgrave, for example, was called upon to produce a design for the funeral car of the Duke of Wellington. An interesting account of this herculean task, completed from sketch design to actuality in just over three weeks, appears in his memoirs [31]. Both were offered knighthoods for their services to art, though Redgrave refused his, preferring his existing humbler station. Both had a share in the training system which developed after 1852, and in the building-up of the South Kensington museum, though it is worth recording that Redgrave, always a modest man, had this to say in his private papers:

> I have no wish to disparage the work of my colleague, Sir Henry Cole, but this I do say, that all that which relates to the building up of the system and the course of Art instruction in our 130 schools and 500 night classes, and the system of teaching and examining both in these and in the public elementary schools of this country, the examination and method of certificating masters, etc., is of my framing. Besides which I have had to be responsible, up to this time, for all the purchases in our rapidly-formed and rich museum. [32]

A final thought on these partners in the formative years of state-directed art training is that they were both well aware that the apparently separate objects of training for artisans and for artists towards academic art must be inextricably mixed. Cole spoke, as the Department of Practical Art came into existence, of the impossibility of educating the designer unless the public, 'those who are to use his works or judge of them, really possess the knowledge and ability requisite to enable them to do so' [24]. Further, he adds:

> My own conviction is, that if it were necessary to choose between two courses for fostering the production of imporved design in manufactures, the education of the public at large or of a special class of artizans, the end would be more readily received by teaching the public aright and convincing it of its ignorance, than by educating the artizan only ... if you lead the public to feel the want of beauty and propriety...I am sure the public will soon demand good designs... [24]

Redgrave, following his chief on the same platform, added:

> Everywhere there is evidence of an awakened desire for art education on the part of the public ... and to guide this desire aright, both as to the designer and the public, is the office of the new Department or Practical Art. [33]

And he rounded off his speech by quoting from Reynolds:

> Invention is one of the great marks of genius, but if we are to consult experience we shall find, that it is by being conversant with the inventions of others we learn to invent, as by reading the thoughts of others we learn to think. [33]

The doctrine, then, is now indeed complicated. More simply, it is that art training for better design in manufactures is not art training in a vacuum. Designers and public must understand better design, and to do this they must know more of art generally, for all art is interlinked. Nor is the introduced precept of Reynolds without significance. Reynolds stood for the enquiring and informed mind, and a respect for the good that has gone before. Moreover, if it is the office and duty of the Department of Practical Art to guide the public aright, it must do so, not only in its libraries and museums, but also in the work of its living artists. It must therefore have artists whose work is beyond mere design for manufactures, and it, and the state which it serves, must play a part in training them. It was a difficult and complex problem, and one of which both Cole and Redgrave were aware. As a result both were willing to have more training geared to academic art entering this practical field than they were sometimes prepared to admit publicly.

Certainly, the statistics of their training achievements are impressive. Between 1852 and 1863 numbers rose astonishingly. In the former year there were 454 students at South Kensington and the Female School, and 2842 students in the 17 provincial schools. In the latter year the provincial schools numbered 90, and the total complement of persons under the Department was 87,330, of whom 71,423 were children in elementary schools who received drawing lessons from a master of the neighbouring school of art [34].

What then did the art syllabus of the Science and Art Directory comprise? An examination of that for 1897 reveals the following divisions for examinations in its 30 closely printed pages:

Freehand Drawing of Ornament in Outline (elementary and advanced)
Model Drawing (elementary and advanced)
Drawing in Light and Shade from a Cast (elementary and advanced)
Drawing on the Blackboard
Geometrical Drawing
Perspective and Sciography (elementary, perspective only; advanced, perspective and sciography)
Historic Ornament
Principles of Ornament (elementary and advanced)
Architecture
Architectural Design
Anatomy
Design (elementary, advanced and honours)
Painting of Ornament
Painting from Still Life
Drawing from the Antique
Drawing the Antique from Memory

Drawing from Life
Modelling from the Cast
Modelling from Life
Modelling from the Antique
Modelling Design (elementary, advanced and honours).

Many of these had been taught in the Royal Academy Schools from the beginning. Such were: model drawing, drawing from a cast, perspective and sciography, architecture and architectural design, anatomy, drawing from the antique and drawing the antique from memory, drawing from life, and modelling from the cast, the antique and the life.

Other subjects from the 1897 list were always given some prominence in the teaching of the Royal Academy Schools, even if they were not actually given subject status. For example, the 1897 Historic Ornament and Principles of Ornament sections contained much on the styles used in ornament of differing periods, and the compositional arrangement of ornament. Such a knowledge was always, within Academy Schools' teaching, considered to be part of the stock-in-trade of the history painter. Many Academician history and subject painters had their own personal collections of antiques, dresses, weapons and similar items, and from the earliest times Royal Academy students were encouraged to study in the armoury of the Tower of London. Or again, much of the 1897 section on design took in the ornamental designs of architecture, which had always been studied in the Academy Schools. Similarly, the 1897 section on the Painting of Ornament comprised many areas of study followed to some extent by earlier Academy students — flowers, foliage and natural objects, still-life groups, landscapes and buildings, human figures and animals. All these had been studied throughout the nineteenth century. Thus it can be seen that there was very little that was new in the syllabus at the end of the century, and the whole is very close to the training emphases found within the Royal Academy Schools a century earlier.

The same sort of conclusion can be reached if one studies the types of work for which gold, silver and bronze medals were given by the Department in 1897. The same sort of categorizing is found there as in the Academy Schools from the beginning. For example, gold medals were given for:

drawing from the nude living model, without background, not less than 24 inches high;

similar drawing from antique statue;

a figure modelled and cast in plaster, about 30 inches high, from a full-size, single, antique statue;

a figure modelled and cast in plaster, about 30 inches high, and so on [35].

What may now be said by way of summary?

In the first place, the emphases of the art curriculum remained largely the same throughout the entire nineteenth century. The similarity between the practices of the state-directed Science and Art Department and the eighteenth-century Royal Academy Schools has been noted. These emphases were on the study of the antique, the life, architecture, perspective and anatomy — indeed, all those essentials which Reynolds had envisaged for the painters of history [36]

Secondly, the attempt to link art training to industry never really succeeded. Perhaps the task was too big, or the fear of the loss of trade secrets too alarming. There were many factors at work here. Certainly, the manufacturers themselves never supported the venture to any extent, and, as has been seen, Cole and his Department were happy to let this sink in importance. Informed opinion towards the end of the century believed that the entire scheme of art training for industry had largely failed. It would be difficult to find a more informed body at this time than the 1884 Royal Commission on Technical Instruction, which had this to say:

> Without depreciating what has been done in this direction by the schools and classes under the auspices of the Science and Art Department in this country, and whilst fully alive to the importance of the organisation which tends to the diffusion of art instruction over a wide area, Your Commissioners cannot conceal from themselves that fact that their influence on industrial art in this country is far from being so great as that of similar schools abroad. This is due, no doubt, to some extent to the want of proper and efficient preparation on the part of the students, owing to the inadequate instruction they have received in drawing in the elementary schools. [37]

Thirdly, precept and hard work remained the standards throughout the century. There was a constant exhortation to look to the works of great artists, and there remained the Reynoldsian emphasis on the value of effort. The belief was sustained that much was possible as a result of sheer hard work and drudgery. It could be argued, of course, that this philosophy is found throughout the whole ethos of nineteenth-century English society. The Victorians believed that hard work — and, frequently, morality and religion — were essential to success. But there was a particular relevance of hard work to the pursuits of the artist. Taking painters as an example, the acquisition of certain skills and knowledge as a result of hard efforts was the common factor in all types of nineteenth-century English painters, be they derivatively classical, romantic, pre-Raphaelite, Nazarene or continental. All in essence retained much of the craft-guild approach. Only in the twentieth century have forms of art become acceptable which do not rely on this obvious discipline and acquisition of skills or knowledge.

Fourthly, there were rules. All work continued to be done under rigid rules and emphatic instruction. Much of that work was in the tradition of the craftsman-copier rather than the creative artist. Indeed, it would be true to say that there was a good deal less creativity and originality in the work of students at the end of the nineteenth century than there had been in that of the Academy students at the beginning of that century. The freedom and variation occasioned by the system of Visitors in the Academy was never equalled in the latter-day schools of the Department of Science and Art. By the end of the century art training was uniform and mechanical. It may have been a very good machine in some ways, but it was certainly not the best system to develop the standards of artistic creativity and individuality which are now so prized.

There were some, of course, who saw the inherent dangers of the system. Heath Wilson, though he cannot be commended for good sense in his capacity as Director at Somerset House, was one of these. In his evidence to the 1864 Select Committee he stated, of the Department's system: 'I am anxious that we should not have a mere system of routine and mannerism generated by one authority operating upon the minds of the whole of the people throughout the country,' and he spoke of 'endless regulations to the local schools which appear to me not sufficiently to consider the wants of those different localities' [38]. Ruskin thundered against the system throughout the years. Ironically, in the light of the present position and reputation of the Royal Academy, a more liberal form of art training and freedom of choice ran through the Academy during the second half of the nineteenth century. This is seen, for example, in the lectures of Weekes in the 1870s. In this section he may very well have been thinking of the straitened system of state training:

Do not fancy, because you are pursuing a particular branch of the arts, that nothing which you may read is valuable but what refers directly to that department. A Sculptor may learn much that will be of service to him by entering discussions on Painting, just as a Painter may gain by understanding the principles of Sculpture. This is not quite believed in, nor acted up to now, as I fancy it ought to be: but I look to the students of the Royal Academy as the future representatives of a time when more liberal opinions will prevail, and more consideration be given to those who, though travelling in a different channel, are tending to the same end in art. [39]

There does seem to have been more liberalism, sheer high spirits, and a sense of pride among the Royal Academy students in the second half of the nineteenth century than there was in the state-directed art schools. This comes out in the autobiographies of Frith, Marks and Leslie, and is reflected in the last speech of Millais at the Academy, shortly before his death in 1896: '...I love everything belonging to it — the casts I have drawn as a boy, the books I have consulted in the library, the very benches I have sat on — I love them all...' [40].

By the end of the nineteenth century art training in England was administratively impeccable. Yearly reports of the Board of Education prove its efficiency in statistics! At heart, however, it was soulless, a dull, grinding discipline towards acquired craft skills and rote learning. Whatever of liberality it had in the 1860s would seem to have been eroded by payment by results and Departmental bureaucracy. The creative element scarcely existed, and it must have been clear that there would be a strong reaction in time. As the twentieth century progressed, that swing became increasingly pronounced. Even as long ago as 1945 Sir Alfred Munnings, then President of the Royal Academy, made his personal protest against the swing, which he and others believed had already gone out of control. On the occasion of the Royal Academy dinner, having persuaded the band to play 'The Boys of the Old Brigade', he then proceeded, with a boisterous Churchill at his side, to lay about Matisse and the Moderns. Finally, he flamed out against his vociferous critics, 'I am President, and I have the right to speak. I shall not be here next year, thank God.' [41] It is strange to compare the twentieth-century artistic chaos and aberration in art training which have followed the channelled order of the last century. There may be signs in our present-day colleges of art that the pendulum is beginning the return swing.

# Notes

[1] For some account of the academies in Europe, see N. Pevsner, *Academies of Art, Past and Present* (London, 1940).

In England, plans for an academy had been drawn up by John Evelyn in 1662, though Kneller's Academy, opened in 1711, was the first which was operative. Hogarth opened one in 1735, in St Martin's Lane. The Dilettanti Society, the Society for the Encouragement of Arts, Manufactures and Commerce (started in 1754) and the Incorporated Society of Artists had connections also with art academies or art training. A useful account of these appears in W.T. Whitley, *Artists and their Friends in England, 1700–1799* (London, 1928), Vol. 1.

The two important Scottish academies should not be forgotten — the Glasgow Academy, begun in 1753, and the Edinburgh Academy for the Improvement of Manufactures, opened in 1760.

[2] For some account of the artistic jockeyings which preceded the founding of the Royal Academy, see Whitley, op. cit.

[3] For a short, informed account of this, see E.K. Waterhouse, *Painting in Britain, 1530–1790* (London, 1953), ch. 16, and photographic plates in the same volume, pp. 122–38 *passim*.

[4] The name given to the practice of portrait-painting in the eighteenth century shows its trade nature. This was 'face-painting', and went along with house-painting, coach-painting, sign-painting, etc.

[5] Many versions of the *Discourses* are available. A comparatively recent one, and one to be recommended, is that in the series by the Huntington Library, California (1959), edited by Robert K. Wark. This edition contains a useful Introduction by Wark. (Line references, given below, refer to this edition.)

[6] Reynolds's *Discourses*, I, 145ff.
[7] Ibid., VIII, 307ff.
[8] Ibid., I, 100ff.
[9] Ibid., IX, 86.
[10] Ibid., IX, 74.
[11] Ibid., III, 106ff.
[12] Ibid., IV and V *passim*.
[13] Ibid., III, 313ff.
[14] Ibid., IX, 76ff.

[15] A School of Painting in the Royal Academy was established in 1815.
[16] W.P. Frith, *My Autobiography and Reminiscences* (London, 1890), p. 23.
[17] W.T. Whitley, *Art in England, 1820–1837* (London, 1930).
[18] Ibid., p. 36. See also information given by Dr Jerome P. Webster, of New York City, in Library of Royal Academy of Arts.
[19] Tom Taylor (ed.), *Life of B.R. Haydon* (London, 1853), Vol. 1, p. 25.
[20] A.M.W. Stirling (ed.), *The Richmond Papers* (London, 1926), p. 12.
[21] *Council Minutes of the Royal Academy*, June 1902.
[22] Unpublished lecture by Haydon, written in 1845 and now in the Library of the Victoria and Albert Museum. Quoted in Q. Bell, *Schools of Design* (London, 1963), p. 45.
[23] G.W. Yapp, *Art Education at Home and Abroad* (London, 1853).
[24] Henry Cole, Address delivered at the opening of the Elementary Drawing School at Westminster, 2 June 1852.
[25] B.R. Haydon, *Correspondence and Table Talk* (London, 1876), p. 446.
[26] *The Journal of Design.* See Bell, op. cit., p. 220.
[27] 1863 Royal Commission on the Royal Academy, *Minutes of Evidence*, para. 1017.
[28] It can be seen from the prospectus of the Royal College of Art, at the end of the century, that it had, in fact, taken over the concepts of the mid-nineteenth-century Department of Science and Art: 'The Royal College of Art is established for the purpose of training Art Masters and Mistresses for the United Kingdom, and for the instruction of students in Drawing, Painting, Modelling, and Designing, for Architecture, Manufactures and Decoration.' See *Science and Art Directory* (1897), p. 357.
[29] 1864 Select Committee on Schools of Art, *Report*, p. viii, taken with references in *Minutes of Evidence*.
[30] Bell, op. cit., p. 257.
[31] F.M. Redgrave, *Richard Redgrave: A Memoir Compiled from his Diary* (London, 1891), p. 103.
[32] Ibid., p. 334.
[33] R. Redgrave, Address delivered at the opening of the Elementary Drawing School at Westminster, 2 June 1852.

[34] 1864 Select Committee on Schools of Art, *Report*, p. iv.
[35] *Science and Art Directory* (1897), p. 30.
[36] Even as late as 1923 the candidates from the Royal College of Art numbered: 289 in drawing; 28 in painting; 12 in pictorial design; and 76 in industrial design. Even to this point in time the emphasis was still on the traditional. See *Board of Education Report* (1922–23), p. 100.
[37] Royal Commission on Technical Instruction, 1884, *Report*, p. 519.
[38] 1864 Select Committee on Schools of Art, *Minutes of Evidence*, paras. 2624–7.
[39] Henry Weekes, *Lectures Delivered at the Royal Academy* (London, 1880), p. 293.
[40] G.D. Leslie, *Inner Life of the Royal Academy* (London, 1914), p. 35.
[41] S.C. Hutchison, *A History of the Royal Academy, 1768–1968* (London, 1968), p. 185.

W. H. BROCK

# Prologue to heurism

In June 1884 an International Health Exhibition was held at South Kensington. In the first week of August, as part of the Exhibition, a very successful International Conference on Education was held in the newly opened City and Guilds of London Technical Institute. It was here, in a section devoted mainly to the consideration of teacher training, that Henry Armstrong first heard the term *heurism* or *heuristic* from the lips of Professor John Meiklejohn. It was here, too, on 5 August, in the section devoted to scientific, technical and artistic education, that Armstrong first began to make public his views on education — a pungently critical, but practical, series of noises that were to emanate from him for another fifty years.

According to Armstrong there were several reasons why there was still comparatively little science teaching throughout primary, secondary and tertiary education in the United Kingdom. The public's ignorance of the educative and utilitarian value of science, said Armstrong, was shared by teachers; consequently, in public schools at least, science was taught only as an inferior, or second-best, subject for classics 'failures'. There was a lack of proper textbooks, practical science was erroneously believed to be expensive and, above all, science teaching methods were thoroughly bad.

Most of these points had been made before Armstrong's day, not least in evidence given to the Clarendon Commission in the 1860s. Some difficulties, like that of arranging for a science syllabus in elementary education when children left school at random ages, had been alleviated by the Education Act of 1870; while doubts which had been expressed throughout the century concerning the educative value of scientific subjects whose contents (compared with classics and languages) altered year by year, had diminished in the face of the emergence of research in the humanities.

Many other reasons for the lack of science education had been suggested: the danger of overloading the syllabus and straining children's minds; the argument that the State had failed to supply enough financial support; the splitting of aims and the random, piecemeal approach to educational reforms; the effect of competitive examinations and the system of paying teachers by their results.

It may be argued that most of the difficulties cited in this list, which might be multiplied, arise in three areas or categories of debate. Firstly, the argument over the introduction of science, or the introduction of *more* science, into the curriculum — whether at the elementary, secondary or tertiary levels. Secondly and thirdly, arguments about *which* sciences should be taught and about *how* they should be taught. To a large extent these discussions formed a prologue to Armstrong's self-imposed mission, and we cannot properly understand the reasons for his successes and failures without analysing them.

This analysis, then, contains the following historical elements:
(1) How should science be taught? Are existing methods sound and effective?
(2) Should science be taught as part of Everyman's education? If not taught, or if taught in an insufficient amount, why, and by whom, was this considered unsound? Moreover, what kinds of arguments were used for the expansion of the science curriculum?
(3) Which sciences should be taught? Are some sciences *better* than others for certain stages of children's development?

I

Assuming that some science was taught during the nineteenth century, what methods of instruction were generally used in schools, colleges and universities? We may distinguish five methods.

1. *The lecture-lesson*

Ideally, as Huxley said in a lecture on zoology teaching, lectures awaken attention, excite enthusiasm, guide students to the salient points of a subject, force students to examine the whole of a subject rather than only those portions they like, and suggest difficulties that they have to master and overcome as their studies progress.

The French chemist and Director-General of Public Instruction, Antoine de Fourcroy, had recommended in 1801 that teachers should improvise their lectures on the basis of tabulated headings which they had previously constructed. These headings were to be printed for distribution to the students. According to Fourcroy this method was already used in German universities. Printed syllabuses were widely used by itinerant lecturers in Great Britain during the eighteenth century and were adopted by some science lecturers and professors at Oxford and Cambridge during the nineteenth century. Printed syllabuses were also an essential part of the teaching system adopted by the Royal Institution and some Mechanics' Institutes.

Huxley's variant was to dictate the major principles that he wished to put over, and then to expound on them − a sort of medieval commentary technique.

A lecture may be distinguished from a lesson by the degree of catechetical or socratic activity which is found in the latter. However, lectures rather than lessons seem to have been used extensively in those schools which practised science teaching in the early nineteenth century. Fortunately, the aridness of the science lecture was sometimes alleviated by the demonstration.

2. *The lecture-lesson demonstration*

The technique of the lecture demonstration − the lecture accompanied by experiments − had been developed by the eighteenth-century itinerant lecturers as well as by lecturers in dissenting academies and the Scottish universities. In the nineteenth century the lecture demonstration was made famous at the Royal Institution under Davy and Faraday, the London Institution under Grove and the Polytechnical Institution under Pepper. Its use in German universities (e.g. Bunsen at Marburg and Liebig at Giessen) led in turn to its use at the Pharmaceutical Society, the Royal College of Chemistry and the South Kensington Schools of Science under Frankland and Huxley.

The lecture demonstration was adopted in a few schools such as Mill Hill, Queenwood, King's Somborne, Rugby and the City of London School. From 1870 onwards, of course, many School Boards employed peripatetic lecturers with portable apparatus. This was the only form of practical science teaching in most schools; but only rarely did pupils have the opportunity to handle the apparatus themselves. At the most they might be allowed to stand around a table and assist the operator in succession.

3. *The object lesson*

The object lesson as originally conceived by Pestalozzi's English disciples did not necessarily provide the opportunity to introduce scientific topics, though, potentially, objects like bread or wood could lead to digressions on botany, agricultural chemistry or even mechanics. In effect, they then became 'conversational lectures' based upon the objects of everyday life and action, and often containing a moral or natural theological tone. In the hands of skilled and original teachers such methods were particularly important at the primary level. There are two well-known examples.

First, the work of Darwin's teacher, the Rev. John Henslow, Professor of Botany at Cambridge and Vicar of Hitcham in Suffolk. During his ministry at Hitcham in the 1840s he used flowers to introduce the village children to botany, forestry and agriculture. But though favourably reported and cited before the Clarendon and Devonshire Commissions, and by Lubbock before Parliament, Henslow's example was not widely copied. His son-in-law, the botanist Joseph Hooker, once exclaimed to Youmans about 'the stupid conservatism of England that not a single thing that [Henslow had done at Hitcham] influenced in the slightest degree a single adjacent parish'. Ironically, Henslow's most significant influence was on the curriculum of a public school. When James Wilson was made to reorganize the science teaching at Rugby in 1864 he went to Hooker for advice. Hooker passed him on to Henslow who taught Wilson botany during a summer holiday. The result was the heuristic teaching of botany to all Rugby boys: flowers as objects.

The second, even more famous example is that of the Rev. Richard Dawes (later Dean of Hereford) in the Hampshire parish of King's Somborne. Dawes's extensive use of lecture demonstrations and of object-lesson homilies on subjects like bread and fire inculcated an extraordinary amount of miscellaneous scientific principles and information into his village schoolchildren. His work was summarized in *Secular Instruction* (1847) which, through its official adoption by the Committee of Council of Education as a training manual, was very influential.

The examples of both Henslow and Dawes led, through Wilson and Huxley, to nature study, physiography and Armstrong's general science.

In the hands of bad teachers, of course, objects were replaced by pictures of objects or reading about objects from textbooks.

### 4. *Textbook and learning by rote*

The unimaginative use of scientific textbooks without practical work was all too common, and to some extent encouraged by the payment by results system of the Department of Science and Art. Some useful and imaginative textbooks existed – for example, Hughes's *Reading Lessons* (1855), and by the 1870s there were the splendid Longman's *Textbooks of Science,* Macmillan's *Scientific Class Books* and *Nature Series,* and Youman's *International Scientific Series.* Before these, however, the general type of textbook writer was best characterized by George Henry Lewes in 1856:

The public thirsts for knowledge; but our men of science are silent, or write only for their brethren, and the consequence is, that where men who are wise 'fear to tred', men who are otherwise rush in with great alacrity. Catchpenny trash fills a void which popular science might so honourably fill.

These four teaching methods were obviously teacher-centred and, despite the scientific apparatus used in the lecture demonstration, they were essentially non-practical. After 1860, when teachers began to be paid by their own and by their pupils' examination results, this non-practical emphasis was only too easily exacerbated. Except in the hands of gifted self-taught teachers like Dawes and Wilson students were not encouraged to think for themselves and the verb 'to cram' began to appear regularly in educational arguments. What, then, of practical science teaching?

### 5. *Practical science*

Practical science teaching in the nineteenth century, as today, could serve a number of functions when performed by the individual student himself. The aim might be heuristic – to allow a pupil to establish or to 'discover' a scientific principle for himself; it might serve an auto-demonstrative function – that is, the pupil was made to repeat an experiment in order to prove a particular point, or to prepare a known chemical compound. The most usual aim, however, was purely a manipulative one; to train the student in the use of laboratory techniques. In practice, then, most of nineteenth-century practical science was concerned with the techniques of chemical analysis.

## II

Analytical laboratories were common on the continent from the seventeenth century onwards in universities, mining academies, or the homes of individuals like Berzelius. Until the 1830s, when science teaching declined in Scotland, there was a good tradition of laboratory teaching at Glasgow under Thomas Thomson, and extramurally at both Glasgow and Edinburgh. In all these cases the essential stimulus to practical teaching was a medical one.

The Scottish example was brought to London by Edward Turner and reinforced by his successor in the Chair of Chemistry at University College, Thomas Graham. By 1845 there were Chairs of Practical Chemistry at both University College and King's College. In London, too, was the huge teaching laboratory of the Pharmaceutical Society (opened 1844) and in Oxford Street, the laboratory of the Royal College of Chemistry (opened 1845), while at Putney since 1840 were the laboratories and general workshops of the Civil Engineering College.

It seems clear, then, that by 1845 there were ample facilities in the metropolis for vocational training in laboratory procedures. By then there was no longer quite the same need for British students to flock to German universities (i.e. Giessen and Marburg) for laboratory training. This interpretation is borne out by the Giessen matriculation records.

During Liebig's tenure of the chemistry chair at Giessen between 1824 and 1852 a total of sixty British students matriculated — a flow which began in 1836 with Thomas Richardson of Newcastle. To this number must be added an unknown number of 'private-status' students like William Charles Henry and William Gregory whose migration seems to have begun slightly earlier than that of the matriculated students. Even if Liebig is generously estimated to have received as many as forty private pupils, it still follows that no more than a hundred British students passed through Giessen in under thirty-five semesters (i.e. 1835–52). It is true that this figure represents the highest number of foreign students who passed through Giessen, but against it might be set the figure of 800 students who passed through the laboratories of the Royal College of Chemistry in its first twenty years (i.e. 1845–65). It must be noticed, too, that very few of these one hundred students took the German Ph.D. degree (perhaps no more than a dozen); most of them merely passed a semester at Giessen as a finishing touch to their medical studies, or as an analytical preliminary to an industrial career. The great attraction of Germany, of course, was an economic one, and a German 'finish' to a British scientific education remained attractive even after 1845 — the peak year for British students at Giessen — on economic grounds. At Marburg in the 1840s, tuition *and* lodgings could be had for as little as £6.5s.0d. per semester. Tuition alone at the Royal College of Chemistry in 1845 cost £25 per annum exclusive of apparatus and chemicals, while a full residential course with laboratory instruction at Putney Civil Engineering College cost about £95 per annum during the same period.

Laboratories there were, then, for relatively expensive vocational studies in science. But with isolated exceptions such as Tulketh Hall, Preston, Queenwood College, or Rugby School after 1859, schools were without such facilities. In 1875 Norman Lockyer was able to report to the Devonshire Commission that only 13 out of 128 endowed schools possessed a laboratory. (As we shall see, this did not represent a true picture of elementary science teaching as a whole since it ignored the schools sponsored by the Department of Science and Art.) Yet by 1902 there were over a thousand school laboratories in Great Britain.

Was this enormous expansion, which was complemented by the growth of non-chemical, but specialized, laboratories in the universities, due to Henry Armstrong's heuristic campaign? Or did Armstrong give voice and strength to a movement that had been begun by his predecessors?

When Edward Frankland (1825–99) replaced the German Wilhelm Hofmann as Professor of Chemistry at the Royal College of Chemistry (which was by then incorporated in the Royal School of Mines) he inherited the task of setting and marking the examinations of the Department of Science and Art. Frankland's examination reports during the 1860s repeatedly showed exasperation at the way in which examinees revealed their total ignorance of *practical* chemistry. By setting special questions on practical chemistry, for example on qualitative analysis, he had hoped to encourage practical work in science classes. (Notice that at this stage no attempt was made to examine their practical knowledge *practically*; it was believed that this could be assessed from written work.) However, far from encouraging real practical work, examinees authoritatively described experiments that they had obviously never seen, or ones which could not possibly work!

Frankland's exasperation and anger had two effects. First, in 1869 he estimated roughly how much it would cost to run a science school laboratory course in chemistry – a minimum of £2 per pupil per ar um – and he then successfully persuaded the Department of Science and Art to provide grants towards the endowment of laboratory facilities in bona fide science classes. Although rather severe restrictions and conditions were imposed by the Government, nevertheless by 1871 many non-endowed schools had taken advantage of the system. In the second place, Frankland saw that it was useless to equip schools with laboratories or to set practical tests of pupils' skills unless the teachers themselves were adept at chemical manipulation. In 1869, followed by Huxley a year later, Frankland began summer schools for teachers in his cramped laboratories in Oxford Street. He worked the teachers hard, in German fashion, from 9.0 a.m. until 5.0 p.m. each day for a week, presenting them with a lecture-demonstration course, and forcing them to work through qualitative analysis and some organic preparations. Out of Frankland's experience came his monograph *How to Teach Chemistry* (edited by George Challoner, a teacher who attended the course in 1872, and published in 1875). This book described the 109 experiments that Frankland believed all pupils should be shown by their teachers. Significantly, these experiments became part of the chemistry syllabus laid down in the *Science Directory* each year. Although Frankland believed in the value of practical work by the pupils themselves, in his courses for teachers he seems to have laid his stress upon the more economical teaching method of lecture demonstration. Nevertheless, through the Department of Science and Art, Frankland introduced practical chemistry examinations for advanced pupils. Until 1892, with John Percy's metallurgy, this was the only practical examination in British non-university scientific education.

This brief account of Frankland's enterprise suggests that practical science teaching was an established aim of some before Armstrong made his prognosis in 1884. In fact, it is possible to distinguish at least four components which together catalysed the increase of practical education during the last three decades of the nineteenth century.

The most important of these elements was a distinctive and deliberate propaganda movement, or pressure group, which advocated laboratory teaching from the 1840s onwards. The epicentre of this movement was a group of nine men who met and dined regularly each month in London and who called themselves the X-Club. (Shades of the eighteenth-century Lunar Society who had also been intensely interested in practical scientific education!) Recent studies in the sociology of Victorian science by Walter Cannon and Roy MacLeod have demonstrated the significance of 'networks' of scientists like the X. Victorian scientific networks shaped and directed the course of scientific activity through the public fronts of scientific societies, the British Association for the Advancement of Science, the universities and other scientific institutions. The X, in particular, were noticeably successful in bringing the issue of science education before these institutions and government itself.

Of the nine members of the X-Club (Busk, Frankland, Hirst, Hooker, Huxley, Lubbock, Spencer, Spottiswoode and Tyndall), six were educationally important. Using their own epithets, they were:

X-centric John Tyndall — physicist: teacher at Queenwood College, deliverer of an important lecture on the teaching of physics at the Royal Institution in 1854, a great adult educationalist, examiner for the Department of Science and Art and the Committee on Military Education.

X-alted Thomas Huxley — biologist: his manifold educational interests and services need no description.

X-haustive Herbert Spencer — philosopher: author of the influential *Education: Intellectual, Moral and Physical* (1861).

X-travagant Thomas Archer Hirst — mathematician and physicist: teacher at Queenwood College and University College School, Professor at University College London, Assistant Registrar of the University of London, Assistant Secretary of the British Association, spokesman for a more practical, anti-Euclid, geometrical teaching, and founder member of the Mathematical Association. His journals reveal a great deal concerning the educational activities of the X.

X-quisite Sir John Lubbock (Lord Avebury) – natural historian: the group's parliamentary spokesman.

X-pert Edward Frankland – organic and physical chemist: teacher at Queenwood, Professor at Owen's College, the Royal Institution and the Royal College of Chemistry, examiner for the Department of Science and Art.

Of these six men, none had been to an English university: but three of them, Frankland, Hirst and Tyndall possessed German Ph.D.s.

The geographical centre for the group was the Royal Institution and the Jermyn Street School of Mines. Since they met monthly in a hotel in Albemarle Street, MacLeod has appropriately called them an 'Albemarle Street conspiracy' boasting considerable experience of foreign lands, and possessed with fixed ideas concerning the place of science in society and the role of science education in securing that place.

Furthermore, it is useful to consider the X as the nucleus of a large educational network spread throughout the British Isles. Surrounding the six were a number of other figures who were either bound to them by ties of individual friendship, or who were intimately connected with the scientific activities of London University and the Department of Science and Art. For example:

Robert Galloway – chemist: teacher at Queenwood College and Professor of Practical Chemistry at the Museum of Irish Industry in Dublin. Author of the perceptive book, *Education, Scientific and Technical* (1881) and the widely used textbook, *The First Step in Chemistry* (1851).

Edmund Atkinson – chemist and physicist: teacher at Cheltenham and Sandhurst, textbook writer.

Heinrich Debus – chemist: teacher at Queenwood College and Clifton College, Professor of Chemistry at the Royal Naval College, Greenwich.

James Wilson – mathematician and clergyman: science teacher at Rugby, author of a distinguished essay on science teaching in Farrar's *Essays on Liberal Education* (1867) and with Hirst the spokesman for anti-Euclidian geometry.

Alexander Williamson – chemist: Professor of Chemistry at University College, London agitator for London University science degrees and a teaching university.

William Benjamin Carpenter — biologist: Registrar of London University.

The network also functioned internationally through the X's friendship with the blind American science lecturer and journalist, Edward Youmans. The latter was the originator of the important textbook venture, the *International Scientific Series*.

Further studies of private correspondence will have to be made before the extent and membership of this network can be defined precisely. Should not Playfair, Hofmann and Roscoe be included, for example? But unless exclusions are made and explained the historical value of the network concept will be lost and one might just as well talk all-embracingly about the pressure exerted by 'the scientists'. It must be shown that although there were other scientists who played roles of educational significance, their work was independent of the network's.

It will be argued, then, that a large network of scientists and scientifically oriented administrators consciously shaped the alteration of existing curricula into ones which included science as a respectable branch of education; furthermore, that the network was especially concerned to inject *practical* science into the curriculum.

As is well known, it was pointless to argue in the nineteenth century that science must be taught because it is vocationally useful (though this is what Spencer argued), since most people in schools and universities did not believe that professional training was the purpose of education. The subjects that were included in the curriculum were justified as being educationally 'right' or 'sound'. Clearly, the task of the network was to establish that science was educationally sound and a valid and important branch of human training. In a nutshell the network's argument was: 'anything you can do with classics and geometry we can do as well, if not better, with science'. Less extreme was the view: 'there are many things you cannot inculcate with classics and mathematics which can be taught by science'.

The supporters of 'liberal education' had traditionally argued that classics and mathematics would train the mind sufficiently for any future career. Similarly, the members of the network argued that the sciences were also mind-training; above all, that science was a mental discipline that required exact and accurate observations. The discipline of science cultivated the ability of 'reasoning towards causes' (Faraday), the power to group and classify phenomena and to generalize from them. According to Spencer and Tyndall, an education in the sciences trained memory, understanding, judgement, observation, morals, sincerity and even religion.

The network's arguments have often been discussed by historians of education. However, two fascinating aspects of this mid-Victorian discussion have tended to be overlooked. In the first place the network found some powerful ammunition for its campaign from the wave of superstitious fads and fancies that swept through Europe, and especially Great Britain, during the 1850s and 1860s. Table-turning and miraculous séances were criticized by Faraday, Tyndall, Carpenter and others; because men were uneducated in the methods of the sciences they lacked critical judgement and became the dupes of frauds and self-deception. The Clarendon Commissioners heard much from the scientists concerning science and judgement and mass hysteria.

Secondly, it is to be emphasized that the whole debate over scientific education took place within the context of faculty psychology. Here is Armstrong in 1884 echoing the arguments of the fifties and sixties: '[Science] tends to develop a side of the human intellect which ... is left uncultivated even after the most careful mathematical and literary training: the *faculty* of observation and of reasoning from observation and experiment.' (My italics.) The conception of choosing a curriculum that would train and stimulate each civilizing faculty originated in the phrenological movement, and especially with George Combe. Many of the members of the X-Club, such as Tyndall, Hirst, Spencer and Frankland, had been exposed to educational ideas derived from phrenology in their youth.

Armed with its arguments for the educative and faculty-training functions of the sciences, the network found further ammunition for its cause in economic considerations: namely, the urgency with which various government Commissions made unfavourable comparisons between education and industrial output in other countries – notably Germany. Needless to say, the members of the network themselves provided some of the more alarming evidence (e.g. Frankland at the Taunton Commission in 1867, PP. 1867 [3898] xxvi, pp.12–13).

III

However, the network's campaign was less efficient and successful than it might have been because of its indecision, lack of policy, or lack of agreement on which sciences should be taught and at which educative stages they would be most effective. They agreed that liberal education would be improved with the addition of science to the curriculum, and they agreed that the nation's industry and wealth would be improved if the faculties were trained through practical observational sciences like botany, natural history, chemistry and physics. But did all these sciences have to be taught? Were some educationally more useful than others? How much science had to be taught compulsorily prior to matriculation?

Here was plenty of room for disagreement, and scientists outside the network could cause further confusion. For example, when the Clarendon Commissioners were faced with a contradictory mass of evidence from the scientists (network and non-network) they ended up by concluding that the biological sciences and the physical sciences appealed to different faculties, but that only discussion and experience would reveal which should be studied first. In fact, one scientific party had suggested that the physical sciences laid the foundation for the study of the biological; but many physical scientists haughtily dismissed the biological sciences as less scientific than either physics or chemistry. Botany was only suitable for young ladies!

The reasons for this disagreement are not hard to find. The progress of the individual sciences in the nineteenth century and their oscillating popularity was bound to have educational ramifications — the century began fashionably with chemistry, followed by geology and biology, and ended with the excitement of physics. Moreover, the Victorians' philosophical obsession with the classification of the sciences (e.g. Comte and Spencer) seemed to imply that there existed a natural hierarchical order of study; but which system was right?

The most consistent policy ever to emerge came from the British Association's Committee on Scientific Education in 1867. Created by Farrar, their report (which was published as a White Paper) was written by Tyndall and Wilson (not by Huxley, as often stated). Privately, however, even they disputed over the role of chemistry in education, though publicly they agreed to say that elementary chemistry should be studied in advanced courses. (Needless to say, there was no chemist on the committee!) Their philosophical agreement with the Combean distinction between courses of *scientific information* (positive instruction) and those of *scientific training of the faculties* (instrumental instruction), led them to the practical conclusion that there was a common core of factual information covering the laws and phenomena of the universe (cf. Dawes) that should be an essential part of everyone's education. Here were the seeds of Huxley's famous programme of physiography, Wilson's highly successful course at Rugby, and the 'Science for All' campaign of this century. Upon this general science base would be built the more intensively studied, faculty-broadening subjects of experimental physics, elementary chemistry and botany. It is not clear from their report, however, whether all three subjects were to be studied, and in any case the report was never directly implemented, and not all members of the network seem to have agreed with it.

The network was unanimous that positive instruction in the sciences should be given to young children, certainly from the age of ten onwards, though it will be recalled that the Clarendon Commissioners failed to recommend science as an element of the Common Entrance examination. As might be expected, the individual members of the network had different ideas concerning the number of hours which should be devoted to science in a school curriculum. On average they recommended between four to six hours per week; this included preparation and laboratory time. Lubbock, who made an elaborate survey of headmasters and individuals asking them what their ideal science week would be (assuming a 38-hour week) had answers that ranged from two to ten hours a week. It was notably the scientists who wanted more than the headmasters' average of four hours a week.

The network's failure to speak with a united front on the minutiae of educational practice was the key to Armstrong's success. He provided syllabuses, he provided a curriculum, he switched the network's arguments about *why* science should be taught to *how* it should be taught, from arguments about the merit of individual sciences to the value of scientific method *per se* and the importance of acquiring certain skills of measurement and concepts like conservation. Above all, he spoke as one man with an unequivocal voice.

Yet it is important to notice that Armstrong himself was an heir to the network's activities — the prologue to heurism — for he was intimately tied to it through his training under Frankland at the Royal College of Chemistry. Frankland, whom Armstrong subsequently hero-worshipped, had been introduced to science by *Sandford and Merton* and Jeremiah Joyce's Edgeworth-inspired *Scientific Dialogues*. His commitment to practical training in science was reinforced by his experience as a druggist's apprentice in Lancaster and by the study of the German teaching methods of Bunsen at Marburg and Liebig at Giessen. As a young man Frankland had seen the value of practical science for the education of children at the extraordinary Quaker school of Queenwood College in Hampshire and, as we have seen, he used his position as an examiner for the Department of Science and Art to encourage practical chemistry in British science schools. From Frankland, then, Armstrong learned the value of practical science. Moreover, Armstrong received his postgraduate training from Frankland's closest friend, the German sceptical chemist, Hermann Kolbe. Kolbe reinforced Frankland's teachings and gave Armstrong a healthy — perhaps too healthy — philosophical scepticism of any current orthodoxy, whether in science or in education.

Faced at last with classes of his own to teach — medical students at St Bartholomew's hospital and adults at the London Institution — he was horrified by their lack of practical ability and by their mental inertia. The problem now, he realized, was not so much to expand science teaching by the methods the old network had used. Quantity did not mean quality. Instead, methods of instruction had to be revolutionized. Armstrong's solution, the hitherto little-practised heuristic method, was rendered acceptable to educationalists by his badgering of the Chemical Society, the British Association, and the Department of Science and Art; and above all, by his demonstration of its practicability with his own children and the boys of Christ's Hospital.

## BIBLIOGRAPHY

*Note*: A more detailed and annotated version of this paper will be given in a history of scientific education by W.H. Brock and A.J. Meadows (in preparation). Here only a brief bibliography will be given.

H.E. Armstrong, *The Teaching of Scientific Method* (London, 1903)

W.F. Cannon, 'Scientists and Broad Churchmen: an Early Victorian Network', *J. British Studies,* Vol. 4 (1964), pp. 65–88

Rev. R. Dawes, *Suggestive Hints Towards Improved Secular Instruction* (London, 1847, 1848 and 1849)

J.V. Jensen, 'The X Club: Fraternity of Victorian Scientists', *Brit. J. Hist. Sci.,* Vol. 5 (1970), pp. 63–72

J.A. Lauwerys, 'Herbert Spencer and the Scientific Movement' in A.V. Judges, *Pioneers of English Education* (London, 1952)

*Lectures on Education Delivered in the Royal Institution* (London, 1855)

Sir J. Lubbock, *Addresses, Political and Educational* (London, 1879), Essay III

R.M. MacLeod, 'A Victorian Scientific Network: the X-Club', *Notes and Records Royal Society,* Vol. 24 (1969), pp. 305–22

D. Thompson, 'Queenwood College, Hampshire', *Annals of Science,* Vol. 11 (1955), pp. 246–54

A. Sutcliffe, 'Students' Laboratories in England: A Historical Sketch', *School Science Review,* Vol. 11 (1929–30), pp. 81–90

A. Wankmüller, 'Ausländische Studierende der Pharmacie und Chemie bei Liebig in Giessen', *Deutsche Apotheker-Zeitung,* Vol. 107 (1967), pp. 463–6; available also as a Sonderdruck, Tübinger Apothekengeschichtliche Abhandlungen, Heft 15, Deutscher Apotheker Verlag (Stuttgart, 1967)

E.L. Youmans, *Modern Culture* (London, 1867)

R.M. Young, *Mind, Brain and Adaptation in the Nineteenth Century* (Oxford, 1969)

E. G. EDWARDS

# The need for a history of higher education

I would like to examine some contemporary problems of higher education in the hope that you might be able to judge the extent to which historical research could illuminate them. I suppose that for the layman the value of history is its capacity to help him to define and contain the present and perhaps its extension into the future. Not that he should expect it to enable him to predict the future; rather the opposite, that it might free him from that determinism, even fatalism, which results from the naive over-simplification of history — that backward projection of prejudice and ignorance which creates a false sense of the permanence of what is merely present custom or fashion in thought or in social institutions.

I would hope that history would prepare us for surprise in the nature of the movement of society through time, just as science prepares us for surprise in the nature of the physical or animate world, and art prepares us for surprise in our sensibility of the significance of living and acting in it. When I say preparation for surprise I might alternatively say preparation for creative activity which arises from the private shock of a new vision of the nature of things and manifests itself by converting a private vision into a social illumination.

I say preparation for surprise because without such preparation (which may be regarded as the role of education itself) surprise comes merely as a shock and we attempt to incapsulate the new within the limitations of the past.

In the field of higher education I select three interconnected contemporary problem areas where the practice of the immediate past appears subject to severe challenge:
(1) The expansion of student numbers
(2) The problem of specialization
(3) The problem of the relevance of higher education to social practice.

# THE CHANGING CURRICULUM

## I

There is a current mythology that the rapid expansion of higher education is a very recent process in which reluctant universities have sacrificed their standards to social pressures. The data about student enrolments in higher education in the UK have not been properly collated; indeed they hardly exist in comprehensible form. The statistics in the USA are firmer. Between 1900 and 1960 full-time enrolments expanded from 240,000 to 3,500,000. What is particularly interesting is that the expansion for 60 years followed almost exactly

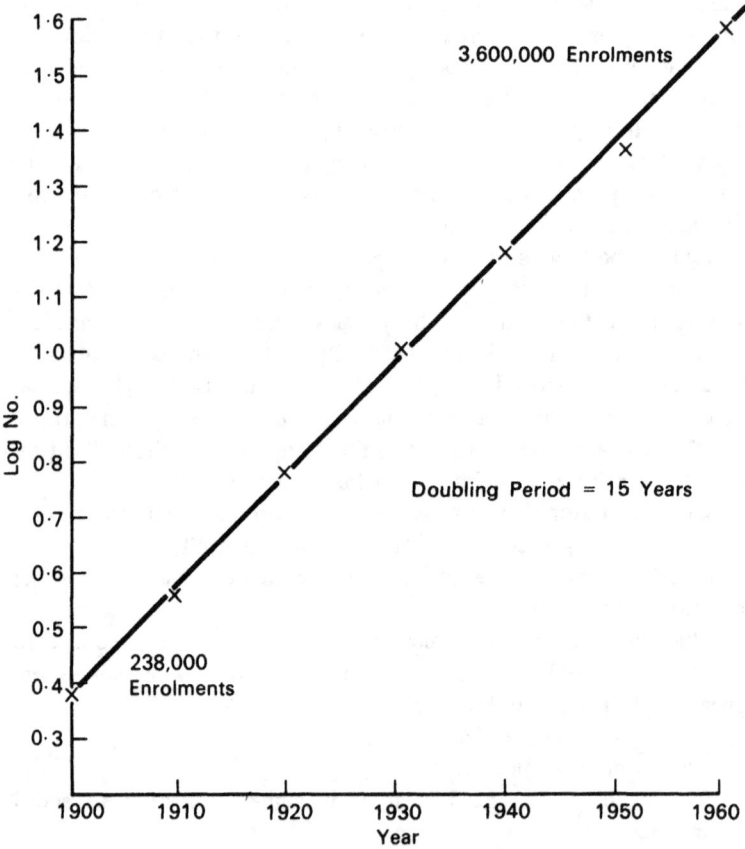

Fig. 1. Expansion of full-time higher education in the USA

an exponential curve with a doubling period of 15 years. Fig. 1 shows log enrolments plotted against time. The UK statistics are much less reliable but the best estimates I have been able to make are given on Fig. 2. In spite of irregularities probably associated with the two world wars and their aftermaths, the line is reasonably linear with a doubling period of slightly longer, i.e. 16–17 years.

It would be interesting to plot similar data for other advanced countries. From their total enrolments in 1960 one would expect broadly similar processes.

Now the Robbins proposals for expansion in the seventies postulated a doubling period of about 15 years, i.e. the postulated figure of 344,000 in 1970 becomes 697,000 by 1985. This would be no faster a rate of exponential expansion than that established since 1900 in the

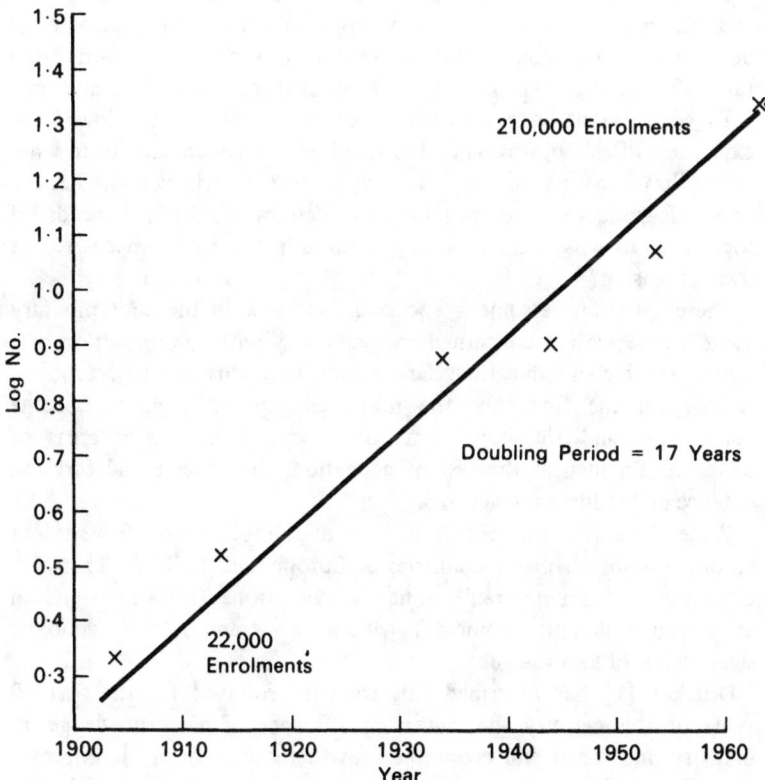

Fig. 2. Expansion of full-time higher education in England and Wales

USA and only slightly faster than that established for the same period in the UK.

In spite of these apparent long-term secular trends one would suppose that the expansion of higher education is in reality a very complex process. In terms of modern systems analysis it would be a multivariant feedback system affecting and being affected by the expansion and quality of secondary education, the social demands for graduates, the economic and educational policies of governments, local authorities and the higher educational institutions themselves.

However, it is tempting to relate the expansion of higher education to another process which has probably followed an exponential curve of expansion in this century – the expansion of objective knowledge. The doubling period of this process has been of the same order, 12–15 years, as that for enrolments in higher education.

To what extent have these processes of the expansion of knowledge and the expansion of the knowledge industry (higher education) been quasi-autonomous like chain reactions in which for a period the rate of reaction is practically independent of external conditions?

To what extent has the expansion of higher education followed the expansion of school leavers of the required entry standards or to what extent has it generated the latter expansion? To what extent has the flow of graduates into society been determined by the needs of society or to what extent has it generated in society the needs for its own expansion?

These questions assume a special importance in the contemporary scene where we are concerned in a new way with the formation of a policy for higher education. One reason why this is a new problem is that for the first time the resources required begin to become comparable and therefore competitive with other major areas of consumption such as the rest of education, the other social services, defence and industrial investment.

Table 1 shows the contemporary doubling periods for student enrolments in the major countries of Europe and the USA. There are clear signs of a new trend, a new acceleration. This new trend in expansion apparently coincides with a new trend in the economic significance of knowledge.

Drucker [1] has described this trend as follows: for the first 60 years of this century the increasing influence of new knowledge on industry and social and economic growth resulted from the improvements it made possible in existing industries, most of which had been essentially established in their present form in the decades preceding the turn of the century.

Doubling Period of Total Student Enrolments in Higher
Education in the Period Immediately Prior to 1966.

|  | To the nearest whole number in years |
|---|---|
| United States of America | 10 |
| United Kingdom | 9 |
| France | 9 |
| West Germany (university-level only) | 10 |
| Italy (estimate) | 10 |
| Norway (university area) | 6 |
| Sweden | 6 |
| Denmark | 8 |
| Belgium | 10 |
| Netherlands | 9 |
| Yugoslavia | 8 |
| Greece | 6 |
| Turkey | 7 |
| Austria | 8 |
| Spain (university-level only) | 16 |

In the second half of the century the essentially new trend is the emergence of a new kind of industry primarily created by the knowledge explosion. Electronics, plastics and man-made fibres, computers and information systems of all kinds, are the typical examples.

The universities and centres of higher education move from the periphery of the economy towards the centre. New industries group themselves around the universities or around their products, knowledge or graduates. Whereas until recently the universities considered themselves subject to pressures from society, they now become the major source of pressure on society.

More importantly still, the previously accepted objective of industrial societies, the accumulation of material wealth, begins to fall into place as an objective with a limited historical validity. When knowledge itself becomes the major product of industry the old dichotomy between culture and material prosperity assumes a new form.

Currently we are debating the expansion of higher education in the 1980s. The Robbins calculations (six years after the report) are already seen to be enormous underestimates [2]. What were the reasons for such miscalculations? To what extent were they attributable to that incapacity for surprise (latent in his appendices but suppressed in the report itself) which may be a consequence of the lack of a modern history of higher education?

The reaction of the establishment (government, civil servants, university hierarchies) to the new projections betrays all those characteristics of unprepared surprise which can only face the challenge of the new with the limited outlook of the past. The list of possible economies and retrenchments being considered would be relevant to a poor country threatened by a crop failure rather than an advanced country challenged by the revelation of enormous new potential assets. The real problem is to realize the assets. The really urgent question is not economies within the sphere of higher education (important though it is to reduce real wastage of resources). It is rather to plan for the reception by the institutions of higher education, industry and society of the new talents, to make sure that they are not wasted or frustrated by lack of preparation for their utilization.

II

This leads me to the second area of present debate in higher education, the nature of the curriculum and the nature of preparation for it in the schools. In the case of the universities the problem of specialization versus generalization has been the subject of a number of major reports. The Robbins Report [3] reflected on it. The Hale Committee [4] flirted with it. The Dainton [5], Swann [6] and McCarthy [7] reports dwelt specially on the aspects in the fields of science and technology.

Currently the Schools Council (with the partial support of the Standing Conference on University Entrance) has published its proposals for the reform of sixth-form curricula and examinations. I say with the partial support of S.C.U.E. since, contrary to customary belief, it is apparently not the universities who are pressing for the retention of sixth-form specialization. The university side wanted five subjects spread through both years of the sixth-form. It is the school side which is apparently insisting on three-subject specialization being retained in the final year.

In the debate it is generally assumed that everyone understands what is meant by specialization. It is usually equated with the production of specialists. It is assumed that it is achieved by concentration on a small number of subjects of study and that the definition of the subjects is well understood. Finally, it is assumed that there is a natural tendency for specialization to get even more specialized so that increasingly scholars, researchers, practitioners will know more and more about less and less.

It is generally assumed that specialization in academic study is associated with what is called depth, which is contrasted with the superficiality of broader studies. On the other hand, in the world of practice, of industry, specialization is associated with a fragmentation of the processes of production and a dehumanization of labour, the conversion of men into robots.

Now all these assumptions have a certain degree of validity. To what extent are they permanent features of human discovery and practice arising from some inevitable and predetermined characteristics of the processes of discovery and practice or to what extent are they temporary, merely arbitrary and somewhat crude descriptions of a particular historical period? It is perhaps worth noting that whereas the verb 'to specialize' is a seventeenth-century word, the noun 'specialist' is given the date 1862 in the Oxford Dictionary. The distinction is interesting. Specialization does not necessarily imply the specialist, i.e. someone who is confined to a particular area of specialization.

If we focus attention on the existential momentary act of investigation, then specialization appears as the necessity to use increasingly sophisticated techniques and we may conceive the specialist as a master of a small number of these techniques. On the other hand, the validation of discovery always depends on establishing the significance of what is discovered in relation to the network of knowledge or practice other than itself. The two processes are not alternative, but complementary.

The great advances in science of our time always demonstrate this complementary nature of specialization and the illumination it provides to much broader fields of knowledge. The discovery of the nature of the genetic code by the application of extremely sophisticated techniques of structural physics to the complex world of the living organism is an outstanding example that could be multiplied many times.

But the realization that this fusion of historically separate disciplines is the essence of modern discovery is only recently beginning to affect the organization of scientific research. The major problem of strategy in science is the selection of fields of investigation. The explosion of knowledge and the explosion of the costs of big science mean that this cannot any longer remain a spontaneous process. Weinberg, the

Director of Oak Ridge, one of the largest research institutes in the world, has suggested that the principle of selection in fundamental research must be the likelihood that a research started in one field will have significant repercussions in fields *other* than that in which it started [8]. This is the reverse of the commonly held notion of the direction of specialization in scientific research.

The division of learning and discovery into a series of separate subjects is a historical phenomenon. To what extent does this division assist and in what circumstances does it impede the very intellectual progress from which it arose?

Ben-David has examined the sociology of the scientific professions and the departmentalization of knowledge to which they correspond [9]. They tend to create paradigms of the nature of objective knowledge, discovery and application which may well reflect a rationalization of a professional role-consciousness and a tendency to preserve the conceived role, rather than characteristics permanently inherent in the nature of knowledge or discovery. We may suppose that we will never escape entirely from a tendency to organize knowledge, indeed to discover it, in terms which serve the individual or social purposes of the discoverers. Our very discovery of order in nature may well reflect the human need for order in society.

Because the major strategic problem for research is that of selection of fields of research, a history of specialization in research could be of enormous value in dispelling illusions of its nature and hence freeing us from a preconceived determinism in science. Such a history would be a history of the development of the separate disciplines, of the interactions between them, of the incapsulation of the disciplines in social forms, of the resistances developed to interdisciplinary growth (the case of chemical engineering would be an excellent recent example), of the effect of industrial application on interdisciplinary processes. To write such a history it may be that the historian would have to learn something of the methods of most modern technologies such as industrial dynamics and systems analysis because what he would be dealing with would be a multivariant feedback system.

If the departmentalization of knowledge originates in research, how far, and with what justification, is this projected back into learning, into the curriculum? How far has the high specialization in undergraduate studies in British universities been dominated by a departmental structure in which they become the appendages of the research departments? How far is specialization in the sixth forms a phenomenon of the sociology of the scientific professions? How far does it reflect the role-consciousness of the sixth-form master not so much as a teacher but as a member of a profession where status is equated with highly specialized research?

The situation is even more aggravated if the concentration on subject-specialized education reflects the style of previous research rather than the increasingly dominant modern trend of interdisciplinary research.

We may picture the creative art whether in knowledge-discovery or in application, organization, decision-making or any other sphere of practice as some form of breakthrough to new thinking or method, usually by focusing attention on a single key problem, experiment or step in a theoretical chain. On the other hand the significance of such invention is in the breadth of illumination it gives over a wide field. The significance of learning a particular subject is precisely the illumination it gives to general understanding. From this point of view the curriculum in a specialized field should provide the minimum factual knowledge required to enable the subject to be used as a creative tool and the maximum understanding of its relation to other fields.

A history of education might trace the ebb and flow of the processes of memorizing facts or of finding relations, essentially purposive uses for factual knowledge.

Indeed, perhaps we can only reform our conceptions of the nature of the learning process by re-examining the relation between learning and practice, knowledge and its application. To what extent does the extreme specialization of the past century coincide with the idea of the pursuit of knowledge for its own sake?

III

The problem of the relation of education to practical application is the third crucial problem of present policy in higher education. The debate here is the significance and justification of the binary system. The binary system is a historical fact. Curiously enough it is a peculiarly English phenomenon. Germany, of course, has its Technische Hochschulen and France its Écoles Supérieures but these are institutions more akin to Imperial College or M.I.T., than the public sector in English further education.

To what extent is its continuance a long aftermath of the early dominance of England in the Industrial Revolution which was created, not by scientists or university graduates, but by practical, largely self-taught engineers?

The philosophy of the binary system is based on the assumption that there are two separable roles for higher education. The first and most prestigious is the pursuit of knowledge for its own sake which is the function of the autonomous area, subject to the minimum social control. The second is the pursuit of knowledge for the sake of its application which is the aim of the public, socially responsible, state-controlled sector.

The key missing part of the policy for higher education in 1980 is the division of future students into these two sections. Is it to be 70:30, 60:40, 50:50, or what? So long as the administration is separate no plans can be elaborated until this question is decided.

On what basis could it be decided?

(1) The new proposals for Q and F levels would tend to a division on a basis of academic attainment, i.e. we might calculate what proportion of students would reach F level and even what proportion might reach a high standard. This method simply perpetuates the historical difference of status between the two systems and makes nonsense of the notion of parity.

(2) On the basis of some estimate of the demand by employers for 'practical' graduates on the one hand as against 'theoretical' chaps on the other. There is no basis for making such an estimate. In any case, in which pocket would the graduates from the technological universities go?

(3) On the basis of taking the existing universities and the nominated polytechnics and colleges of education as the units for graduate-level higher education and optimizing the size of each individual institution in relation to its present spread of work. This might be the most sensible *ad hoc* method of dealing with the problem within the binary system.

(4) The most likely method would be that which provides for the maximum number of students at the minimum cost. Assuming that the public sector does only a fraction of the research work of universities, then their unit costs per student year when stabilized might be below university levels. In effect, the staff would be working longer teaching timetables. This method would maximize the development of the public sector and possibly the whole of the expansion might be planned to be accommodated in that sector.

(5) On the basis of some estimate of the proportions of students who, given free choice, would choose the universities rather than the public sector. This method would almost certainly tend to expand the university proportion far beyond its present value and to maximize costs (if the assumptions made about research in the public sector are true). This method, which would be the democratic method, can

therefore be ruled out.

(6) By asking the universities how many students they will take (on various assumptions about extra facilities) and subtracting this from the total to give the public-sector figure. Whatever the answer given by the universities, the probability is that they will in fact take on as many students as they possibly can; again assuming that this is the way for them to get extra resources. Despite their occasional demure disclaimers, most universities have a tremendous appetite for expansion since it is the most painless way of securing provision for the innovation that they must accommodate. Otherwise they would have to cut out dead wood and no university has any notion how to do this.

Other methods of arriving at the proportions are possible such as thinking of a number or simply allowing it to be decided by the push-pull process of local and national politics.

One thing is clear: no one has suggested any method which corresponds to the supposedly different philosophy and goals of education of the two systems. This is natural since the supposed difference is probably mythological or reflects a historical accident rather than a real difference which is relevant to this period of the twentieth century. If the difference were real we should transfer the education of all doctors, architects, lawyers, civil servants, most engineers and an increasing proportion of scientists to the public sector. Of all students who graduate, only a very small proportion (and a decreasing proportion as student numbers increase) will find their careers in the most abstract research or in scholarship where the connection with the practical application of knowledge is too distant to be taken into account.

On the other hand, industry, the most applied sector of graduate employment, is increasingly making clear that it does not require graduates who are trained for particular practical tasks (except precisely in those areas of quasi-fundamental research where the traditional pure science degree is required).

Industry mainly requires as graduate employees, flexible people who are able to turn their intelligence to problems where new techniques have to be evolved, rather than men already cast in a particular technical mould. On the other hand, it requires a motivation towards application and the capacity to appreciate the complex nature of application from virtually all its graduates. The same is probably true of almost all potential employers of graduates.

The requirement from higher education in a world in which it is increasingly moving to the centre of gravity of the economy and social development is not for more specialized, more technically expert graduates, but for more generalists, more people able to control and manage the increasingly rapid obsolescence of industrial and economic processes, and guide the emergence of new processes.

The nineteenth-century dichotomy between the pursuit of knowledge for its own sake and the application of knowledge becomes historically irrelevant. We could express this by a philosophy of education with the major premise that

> Knowledge is always pursued for the purpose of its application.

This is another way of stating that particular knowledge is always validated, given significance, by something other than itself which is in effect its field of application.

To avoid the charge of crude materialism, I should state that the parallel dialectical equation would be that

> Practice is always pursued for the purpose of adding to knowledge.

I cannot argue this here, but I would like to trace its justification from the thinking of modern structural anthropology (trade as a form of communication), and from philosophical considerations of the role of material progress in liberating and expanding human consciousness. The social problem is, of course, the distribution and dissemination of the expanded culture made possible and given new content by technological advance.

Consideration of the expansion of higher education in the next decade thus focuses attention on three interconnected problems.

(1) The problem of what factors if any should limit the expansion itself and should determine the proportions of students entering various forms of higher education.

(2) The problem of the curriculum: the balance of specialized studies as we presently conduct them and new forms of more general studies.

(3) The problem of the justification for the binary system of higher education which in the longer term becomes the question of whether a comprehensive system of tertiary education is conceivable and practicable.

The actual solution of these problems will, of course, be achieved by a series of more or less disconnected pragmatic decisions taken by more or less disconnected groups of decision-makers. The first approach of the Ministry is based on the assumption that as a country we cannot afford the expansion which seems to be spontaneously generated. Hence the present discussion on the thirteen possible ways of economizing on quantity or quality. But what determines what we can afford on education? Certainly our national resources are not endless and the spontaneous expansion would accelerate the costs at a faster rate than the growth of the G.N.P. But what determines that the proportion we spend on education should not rise at such a faster rate? Would the electorate not be prepared to afford it at the sacrifice of the rate of expansion of other forms of consumption? If they were to be asked, how could the relevance of the expansion of higher education to them be justified? What indeed is that relevance? What historical picture could we give of its development?

The problems of the content and forms of higher education are likely to be determined by the role-consciousness of the various controlling groups in ministries, universities, colleges and local authorities. But how has that role-consciousness arisen? To what extent is it a temporary historical accident?

I have suggested earlier that we are approaching a period in which the pursuit of knowledge and the pursuit of other social and industrial goals begin to stand in a new relationship to each other. In economic and industrial life this is signalized by the growth of tertiary industry. Commerce between the advanced countries becomes increasingly the trading of knowledge, of systems of thought and communication, of theoretical models, rather than trade in material artefacts. The social problem becomes increasingly that of coping with the knowledge explosion and its social effects. Social unrest is concentrated in a new way in the universities and colleges. Though militant students may adopt the slogans of earlier revolutions and the ideologies of a past historical period, student unrest feeds on the uncertainty of their own future, on a basic failure of confidence in what they imagine will be their own future roles.

Can we construct a new philosophy of education against which our pragmatic solutions to its expansion could be tested? Is such a unified philosophy indeed desirable or would it contain inevitably its own dangers to the freedom of thought and invention? The concept of education as a preparation, an apprenticeship, breaks down as the period required lengthens towards the whole of life. The concept of education as a self-justifying experience provides no answer to the problems of its content and forms. The alternatives of whether education should be designed to develop the individual or to fit him to serve economic and social needs stand in an apparent opposition between which the solution is purely arbitrary.

Parallel to these problems within education itself are the questions whether education is to be justified by its contribution to social progress (e.g. economic prosperity) or whether economic advance is to be justified by its provision of education (or more generally by the extent to which it raises the quality of consciousness, the culture, the sensibility and sense of purpose of men in society).

This is not the occasion to attempt to outline an approach to a new philosophy of education and in particular of higher education, the fusion of education with discovery. But the new relationship between knowledge and its application that I have spoken of makes the seeking of such a philosophy a task of primary significance. For such a philosophy to serve its purpose it would have to contain in a new way concepts which at present stand in confrontation and apparent contradiction with each other.

This polarization of concepts tends to be frozen into inflexible rigidity because they are foreshortened in time. We need a deeper historical perspective to reveal the extent to which our thinking is based on dogma rather than on a perception of the real role of education in our time.

# Notes

[1] P.F. Drucker, *The Age of Discontinuity* (Heinemann, 1969).
[2] The latest projection by the Department of Education and Science envisages 727,000 students in full-time higher education in England and Wales by 1981–2 compared with the Robbins projection of 510,000.
[3] *Higher Education,* Cmnd. 2154 (H.M.S.O., October 1963).
[4] University Grants Committee, Report of the Committee on University Teaching Methods (H.M.S.O., 1964).
[5] *Enquiry into the Flow of Candidates in Science and Technology into Higher Education,* Cmnd. 3541 (H.M.S.O., February 1968).
[6] *The Flow into Employment of Scientists, Engineers and Technologists,* Report of the Working Group on Manpower for Scientific Growth, Cmnd. 3760 (H.M.S.O., September 1968).
[7] Department of Education and Science, *Science Policy Studies (3): The Employment of Highly Specialised Graduates* (H.M.S.O., 1968).
[8] A.M. Weinberg, 'Criteria for Scientific Choice', *Minerva,* Vol. I, No. 2 (Winter 1963).
[9] J. Ben-David, 'The Universities and the Growth of Science in Germany and the United States', *Minerva,* Vol. VII, Nos. 1–2 (Autumn–Winter 1968–9).

# Index

Académie des Sciences, 37, 42, 45
academies, 29, 37–50
Acts of Parliament:
    Education (1870), 71
Addison, Joseph, 47
agriculture, 23, 29, 31, 45–6, 74
Antique Academy, 52
architecture, 1, 2, 15, 29, 51, 54, 62–4
Ariosto, 14, 15
Aristotle, 4, 10
    *Categories*, 10
Armstrong, Henry, 71–2, 74, 77–8
    81, 83–4
Ascham, Roger, 22
    *The Scholemaster*, 3, 18
astronomy, 14, 27, 38
Atkinson, Edmund, 79
Austria, 91

Bacon, Francis, 7, 15–16, 22–8, 30,
    32, 34, 37
    *Novum Organon*, 34
    *De Augmentis Scientarum*, 23, 25
    *Of the Advancement and Proficience*
    *of Learning*, 23
Bale, John, 13
Banks, Joseph, 41
Banks, Thomas, 54
Barkman, James, 40
Beckmann, Johann, 45–6
Beddoes, Thomas, 40
Belgium, 91
Bell, Quentin, 57, 60, 68
Ben-David, J., 94, 100
Berlin, 43
    Academy of Sciences, 38, 43–4
    Realschul, 45
Bergman, T.O., 41
Bernouilli, Nicholas, 47
Berzelius, 75
Billanovich, Guiseppe, 6, 11, 18
binary system, 95–6
biology, 78, 80, 82
Birmingham, 37, 41
Blumenbach, J.F., 44

Board of Education, 66
    Report (1922–23), 69
Board of Trade, 56, 58
Boccaccio, Giovanni, 7, 9, 14
Boiardo, 14
Bolingbroke, Viscount, 43
Bologna, 10, 12
Bordeaux, 9, 42–3
*Botanic Journal, The*, 48
botany, 1, 8, 15, 37, 41, 73–4, 82
Botticelli, Sandro, 14
Boulton, Matthew, 41
Bramante, Donato, 15
Brandenburg, 37, 38
Brinsley, John, 5
British Association, 78, 79, 84
    Committee on Scientific Education
    (1867), 82
Brussels, 13, 39
Buchanan, George, 1
Bunsen, Robert Wilhelm, 73, 83
Buoncampagno, *Ars Dictaminis*, 10
Burckhardt, Jacob, *The Civilization of*
    *the Renaissance in Italy*, 2, 7
Busch, J.G., 45
Busk, George, 78

Cambridge, University of, 31, 41, 73, 74
Cannon, Walter, 78
Carpenter, William Benjamin, 80, 81
Carlisle, Anthony, 54
Carpue, J.C., 54
Casaubon, Isaac, 1
Casini, Bruno, 12
Celsius, Anders, 40
Cervantes, Miguel de, 15
Challoner, George, 77
Cheltenham, 79
Chemical Society, 84
chemistry, 31, 38, 73, 75, 77, 79, 82
    laboratories, 37, 40, 41
Chester, 60
Chichester, 41
Christ's Hospital, 84
Chrysoloras, Manuel, 12

# INDEX

Cicero, 12, 13, 15
   *De Amicitia*, 3
   *De Officiis*, 3
City of London School, 73
Civil Engineering College, Putney, 76
Clarendon Commission (1864), 71, 74, 81, 83
Clarke, E.D., 41
Clausen, George, 55
Clausthal, 45
Clifton College, 79
Club d'Entresol, 43
coffee houses, 46–7
Cole, Henry, 57–62, 64, 68
Coleridge, S.T., 39, 49
Colet, John, 9
Combe, George, 81
Comenius, Jan Amos, 24–8, 32, 34, 37
   *A Reformation of Schooles*, 25
   *Janua Linguarum Reserata*, 24
   *Orbis Pictus*, 24
   *Via Lucis*, 32
Committee of Council in Education, 59, 74
Common Entrance, 83
Comte, Auguste, 48, 82
*Consuetudinarium Scholae Etonensis*, 3–5, 8, 18
Coqueret, 9
Cordier, Mathurin, 14
Cosway, Richard, 54
Cowley, Abraham, 29, 32, 35
Crell, *Chemisches Journal*, 48
Cronstedt, Axel Frederic, *An Essay towards a system of Mineralogy...*, 41
Cross, J.G., 45
Cutler, Edmund, *Chemical and Physical Essays*, 40
Czechoslovakia, 24

Dainton Report (1968), 92, 100
Dante, 1, 6
Danzig, 39
Darwin, Charles, 74
Darwin, Erasmus, 37, 49
   *The Botanic Garden*, 37
Davy, Humphrey, 73
Dawes, Rev. Richard, 74, 75, 82, 84
Debus, Heinrich, 79
Dell, William, 26, 27, 30, 34
Denmark, 39, 45, 91
Department of Education and Science, 100
Department of Science and Art (formerly of Practical Art), 51, 55, 57, 58, 61, 62, 64, 65, 68, 74, 76–9, 83, 84
Deriabin, Andrei, 45
Desaguliers, J.J., 43, 47

Descartes, René, 22
Devonshire Commission (1872–5), 74, 76
Dewey, John, 48
Diderot, Denis, 42, 43, 49
Dillen, Johann Jacob (Dillenius), 46
Diophantus, 8
Dioscorides, 8, 15
dissenting academies, 33, 40, 73
Dollond, John, 40
Dorat, J., 1, 9
Dresden, 39, 44
Drucker, P.F., 90, 100
Dryander, Jonas, 41
Dublin, 39, 79
Dury, John, 25–31, 33, 34
Dyce, William, 57, 58, 60
Dymock, Cressy, 29, 34

École des Mines, 45
Écoles Supérieures, 95
economics, 29, 38
Edinburgh, 39
   University of, 75
engineering, 43
England, 6, 13, 15, 38, 40, 46, 51, 58, 60
Erasmus, D., 9, 13, 16
   *De Copia Verborum ac Rerum*, 16
Erfurt, 44
Erlangen, 45
*Essays on Liberal Education*, 79
Euler, Leonard, 44
Evelyn, John, 32
Ewart, W., 56

Faraday, Michael, 73, 80, 81
Farrar, F.W., 79, 82
Feltre, Vittorino da, 13
Ficino, Marsilio, 9, 15
Fieldings, the, 47
Filelfo, 12
Florence, 11, 12
Folkes, Martin, 46–7
Fontenelle, B. de, 42, 49
Formey, J.H.S., 44
Fourcroy, Antoine de, 72
France, 6, 14, 15, 38, 40, 42, 43, 45, 52, 91, 95
Francke, A.H., 45
Frankland, Edward, 73, 77–9, 81, 83, 84
   *How to Teach Chemistry*, 77
Franklin, Benjamin, 43
Frederick the Great, 44, 45
Freiburg, 45
French academies, 42–3
Frith, W.P., 53, 66, 68
Fuseli, Henry, 54

Galilei, Galileo, 22

# INDEX

Galloway, Robert:
  *Education, Scientific and Technical*, 79
  *The First Step in Chemistry*, 79
geology, 40, 82
geometry, 79, 80
George III, 51
Gerbier, Sir Balthazar, 29, 35
Germany, 15, 38, 39, 40, 42, 43, 45, 52, 72, 73, 76, 81
  West, 91, 95
Gibelin, Jacques, 43
Gibson, Milner, 58
Giessen, University of, 73, 76, 83, 86
Gilbert, William, 22
Giotto, 1
Glasgow, University of, 75
Gmelin, J.G., 40
Goethe, J.W. von, 45
Goldsmith, Oliver, 47
*Gorboducs*, 2, 17
Göttingen, University of, 44, 46
Great Exhibition (1851), 58
Greece, 52, 91
Gregory, William, 76
Gross National Product, 98
Grove, Sir William Robert, 73
*Guardian*, the, 47
Guarino (da Verona), 12, 15
Guelphs, 39
Guyenne, École de, 16

Haarlem, 39
Hale Committee, 92
  Report (1964), 100
Halifax, 60
Hall, John, 28, 30, 31, 34, 35
  *An Humble Motion to the Parliament of England Concerning the Advancement of Learning*, 31
Halle, 40, 45
Haller, Albrecht von:
  *Elementa Physiologiae Corporis Humani*, 44
  *Königliche Gesellschaft der Wissenschaften*, 44
Hamburg, 45
Harmar, Samuel, *Vox Populi: Gloucestershire's Desire*, 25
Harris, John, *Lexicon Technicum, or a Universal Dictionary of the Arts and Sciences*, 46
Hartlib, Samuel, 25–9, 31, 33, 34
Harvey, William, 22, 27
Haydon, B.R., 54–9, 68
Hecker, J.J., 45
Hegel, G.W.F., 4
Helvétius, 43
Henry, William Charles, 76
Henslow, Rev. John, 74
Herbert, J.R., 57, 58

Hereford, 74
heurism, 71–85
Hiärne, Urban, 40
Hirst, Thomas Archer, 78–9, 81
Hitcham (Suffolk), 74
Hofmann, Wilhelm, 77, 80
Hogarth, William, 47
Hooker, Joseph, 74, 78
Hoole, Charles, 5
Hughes, *Reading Lessons*, 74
Humboldt, Alexander von, 45
Huxley, T.H., 72–4, 77, 78, 82
Huyar, Fausto el, 45

International Conference on Education (1884), 71
International Health Exhibition (1884), 71
*International Scientific Series* (Youmans), 74, 80
Italy, 6, 11, 14, 15, 38, 40, 43, 51, 52, 91

Januensis, Johannes Balbus, 14
Jars, Gabriel, 47
Jonson, Ben, 15, 16
Joyce, Jeremiah, *Scientific Dialogues*, 83

Kepler, Johannes, 22
King's Somborne (Hants.), 73, 74
Klingenstierna, Samuel, 40
Kolbe, Hermann, 84
Kungsholm (Sweden), 40

Lagrange, J., *Mécanique Analytique*, 44
La Lande, J.J. le F. de, 43
Lambin, Denis (Lambinus), 1
Lanarkshire, 47
Lancaster, 83
Laud, William (Archbishop), 30
Laumonier, Paul, 6, 7
law, 10, 11, 29
Leib, Johann Georg, *Probe wie eine Verbesserung Land und Leuten*, 45
Leibnitz, G.W., 38, 39, 44, 48, 49, 50
  *Monadology*, 48
Leipzig, 39, 44, 45
Leopoldine Academy, 38
Leslie, G.D., 55, 66, 69
Levellers, the, 25
Lewes, George Henry, 74
Lewis, C.S., *English Literature in the Sixteenth Century*, 2, 5, 7, 8, 17, 18
Liebig, Justus, 73, 76, 83, 85
Life School, 53
Linnaean Society, 41, 46
Linnaeus, *Systema Vegetabilium*, 41

# INDEX

Lipsius, Justus, 9
Lisbon, 39
Livy, 6
Lloyd, Edward, 47
Lockyer, Norman, 76
Lomonosov, M.V., 45
London, 30, 32, 47, 51, 58, 75
   City and Guilds Technical Institute, 71
   Institution, 73, 84
   School of Design, 56, 58–60, 62
   University of, 78–80
      Colleges: Imperial, 95
                 King's, 75
                 University, 75, 78
Louvain, 13
Lubbock, John (Lord Avebury), 74, 78, 79, 83, 84
Lunar Society, 37, 40, 42, 78
Lyonbergh, Lord, see Barkman, James

Madrid, 39
Malthus, T.R., 41
Manchester School of Design, 58
Manitius, M., 6, 19
Marburg, University of, 73, 76, 83
Margraf, Andreas S., 44
Maria Theresa, 45
Marks, Henry Stacy, 66
Marlowe, Christopher, 8, 15
Marriotte, 43
Marsuppini, 12
Martyn, John, 46
Massachusetts Institute of Technology, 95
Mathematical Association, 79
mathematics, 2, 8, 15, 27–9, 31, 38, 39, 45, 46
   teaching of, 78–80
Matisse, H., 66
McCarthy Report (1968), 92, 100
McLeod, Roy, 78, 79, 85
mechanics, 22, 26
   Institutes, 56, 57, 73
   science of, 26, 31, 73
Medici, Cosimo de', 14
Medicine, 11, 23, 27, 29, 31, 33, 41, 84
Meiklejohn, John, 71
Meneken, Carolus, 13
Merchant Taylor's School, 9
metallurgy, 1, 41
Mexico, 45
Millais, Sir J.E., 66
millenarianism, 22
Mill Hill School, 73
Milton, John, 21, 25, 29
   On Education, 21
*Miscellenea Berolinensia*, 39, 44
Moivre, Abraham de, *Doctrine of Chances*, 46

Montaigne, Michel de, 6, 9, 15, 16
Montemayor, Jorge, de, 15
More, Thomas, 9
Morris, Dr, 47
Munich, 44
Munnings, Sir Alfred, 66

National Gallery, 56
National Collection, 56
*Nature Series* (Macmillan), 74
Netherlands, 13, 45, 91
Les Neuf Soeurs, 43, 50
Newcastle-upon-Tyne, 40, 76
Newton, Isaac, 47
Nicomachus of Gerasa, 15
Nizolio, 9
Northcote, Sir Stafford, 57
Northampton, 46
Norway, 91
Norwich, 41, 60

Oak Ridge, 94
observatories, 38; see also Uppsala
Oliver (Leibnitz's mechanic), 38
Orléans, 10
Otter, William, 41
Ovid, 7
Owens College, 79
Oxford, University of, 25, 30–3, 40, 46, 73
   Wadham College, 30

Paisley, 60
Palladio, Andrea, 15
Palmer, Samuel, 54
pansophy, 24, 25; see also Comenius,, Jan Amos
Paracelsus, Theophrastus, 27
Paris, 43, 44
   Musée de, 43
Parliament, 22, 25, 30, 32, 33, 55, 74
   1653 ('The Saints'), 26
   1835 Select Committee, 56
   1849 Select Committee, 58
   1864 Select Committee on Schools of Art, 56
Pavia, 12
payment by results, 66, 72, 74, 75
Pepper, J.H., 73
Percy, John, 78
Pestalozzi, J.H., 73
Petrarch, Francesco, 1, 6, 9, 11–14, 19
Petty, William, 25–9, 34
Pharmaceutical Society, 73, 75
*Philosophical Magazine, The*, 48
*Philosophical Transactions*, 33, 48
physics, 27, 31
   journals, 48
Pindar, 7

# INDEX

Pisan, Christine de, 8
Plato, 15
Playfair, W.L., 80
Pléiade, the, 2, 6, 16
Pliny, 10
Poliziano, Angelo (Politian), 9, 13
Polytechnic Institution, 73
poor-law reform, 26
Preston (Lancs.), 76
Price, Richard, 40
Priestley, Joseph, 43
   *History of Electricity*, 39
Prussia, 45

Queenwood College (Hants.) 73, 76, 78, 79, 83, 85
Quirino, Lauro, 12

Rabelais, François, 2, 6, 9, 14
Ramsay, the Chevalier, 43
Réaumur, René Antoine Ferchault de, 42, 43
Redgrave, Richard, 59–62, 68
   *Elementary Manual of Colour*, 60
Reform Banquet, 55
Renucci, 11
Reynolds, Sir Joshua, 51–2, 61, 62
   *Discourses*, 52, 67
*Rhetorica ad Herennium*, 9, 12
Richardson, Thomas, 76
Robbins Report (1963), 89, 91, 92, 100
Ronsard, Pierre de, 6, 9, 15
Roscoe, Sir Henry Linfield, 80
Rousseau, J.J., 44
   *Émile*, 44
Royal Academicians, 55, 57, 58, 59
Royal Academy, 51–2, 54–66, 67, 68, 69
   exhibitions, 53
   Schools, 51–63
Royal College of Chemistry, 75–7, 79, 83
Royal Commission on the Royal Academy (1863), 59, 68
Royal Commission on Technical Instruction (1884), 64, 69
Royal Institution, 73, 78, 79
Royal Naval College, Greenwich, 79
Royal School of Mines, 77
Royal Society, 28, 30, 32–4, 37, 40, 46, 48
Royal Society of Arts, 47
Royal Society of Chemistry, 73
Royal Swedish Academy of Sciences, 40
Rozier, *Observations sur la Physique*, 48
Rugby School, 73, 74, 76, 79, 82
Ruskin, John, 65
Russia, 40, 45
Russian Academy of Sciences, 40

Sage, B.G., 45
St Bartholomew's Hospital, 84
St Paul's School, 8
St Petersburg, 39
   Academy, 44
St-Simon, C.H., Comte de, 39, 48
*Sandford and Merton*, 83
Sandhurst, 79
Sandys, J.E., *History of Classical Scholarship*, 6, 19
Sannazaro, 9, 14
Sass, Henry, 53
Savile, George (Marquis of Halifax), 1
Saxony, 45
Scaliger, J.J., 9
Scheele, Carl Wilhelm, 40; *see also* Withering, William
school boards, 73
Science and Art Directory, 62, 69, 77
science teaching, 71–4, 76–9
*Scientific Classbooks* (Macmillan), 74
Scotland, 73, 75
*Secular Instruction*, 74
Semler, Jean Christopher, 45
Shakespeare, William, 6, 15, 16
Shipley, William, 46
Shrewsbury School, 9
Sidney, Philip, 9
   *Arcadia*, 15
Skytte, Bengt, 37
Smith, Thomas, 1
Société Apollonienne, 43
sociology, 38, 78, 94
Solander, Daniel, 41
'Soloman's House', 24, 30, 32, 37; *see also* Bacon, Francis
Somerset House, 56, 58, 65
South Kensington, 56, 59–61
Spain, 45, 91
Spencer, Herbert, 80–2, 84
   *Education, Intellectual, Moral and Physical*, 78
Spenser, Edmund, 9, 15
Spottiswoode, William, 78
Sprat, Thomas, 28, 33, 34, 35
Sprigge, William, 29, 35
Standing Conference on University Entrance (S.C.U.E.), 92
Stein, Frau von, 45
Stevens, Alfred, 58
Stirling, John, 47
Stockholm, 40
Stoke-on-Trent, 60
Strada, Zanobi da, 11
Strassburg, 8
Sturm, Johann, 5, 8, 18, 22
Summerly, Felix, 60; *see also* Cole, Henry
Sussmilch, J.P., *The Divine Order*, 44
Swann Report (1968), 92, 100
Sweden, 37, 39, 40, 42, 45, 49, 91

# INDEX

Tangermünde, 57
Tasso, Torquato, 15
Taunton Commission (1868), 81
Technische Hochschulen 95
*Textbooks of Science* (Longman), 74
Thomson, Thomas, 75
Titian (Tiziano Vecellio), 1
Triewald, Martin, 40
Trondhjem, 39
Tschunkhausen, 39
Tulketh Hall, 76
Turkey, 91
Turner, Edward, 75
Tyndall, John, 78–82

UNESCO, 37
universities, 11, 12, 15, 17, 21, 29, 31, 33, 38, 72, 75, 77, 78, 87–100
Uppsala:
   Academy, 40
   observatory, 40

Valla, Lorenzo, 12
   *Elegantiae*, 14
Vaucanson, 43
Veneto, 11
Vergerio, Pietro Paolo, *De Ingenuis Moribus*, 3, 18
vernacular literatures, 1, 2, 6, 10
   English, 7, 10
   French, 7, 10, 16
   Italian, 10
   Spanish, 10
Vickers, B.W., 7, 19
Victoria and Albert Museum, 56, 68
Vienna, 39, 45
Vinci, Leonardo da, 14
Virgil, 3, 4, 13, 14
'virtuoso', the, 33
Vitruvius, 2
Voigt, Georg, 9, 19
Voltaire, *Micromégas*, 42

Warburg, A., 5
Ward, Joshua, 47
Ward, Seth (Bishop of Salisbury), 35
   *Vindiciae Academiarum*, 31
Wargentin, Pehr, 40
Warrington, 40
Watt, James, 46
Watts, Gilbert, 23
Webster, John, *Examen Academiarum: an examination of the academies*, 31
Weekes, Henry, 65, 69
Weigel, 38, 45
Weinberg, A.M., 93, 100
Weiss, Roberto, 11
Wellington, Duke of, 60
Wells, H.G., 48, 50
Werner, A.G., 45
West, Benjamin, 54
Wilamowitz, Ulrich von, 5
Wilhelmsdale, 45
Wilkins, John (Bishop of Chester), 30–3, 35
   *Vindiciae Academiarum*, 31
Williamson, Alexander, 79
Wilson, Harold, 48
Wilson, Heath, 57, 58, 65
Wilson, James, 74, 75, 79, 82
Winstanley, Gerrard, 25–7, 34
Withering, William, *Scheele's Outlines of Metallurgy*, 40–1
Woodward, Hezekiah, 25
Wurms, F.Ch., 45
Württemberg, Duke of, 39

X-Club, 78–81, 85

Yapp, G.W., 56, 68
Youmans, Edward, 74, 80, 86
Yugoslavia, 91

Zincke, G.H., 45
zoology, 1

For Product Safety Concerns and Information please contact our EU
representative GPSR@taylorandfrancis.com
Taylor & Francis Verlag GmbH, Kaufingerstraße 24, 80331 München, Germany

www.ingramcontent.com/pod-product-compliance
Lightning Source LLC
Chambersburg PA
CBHW071823230426
43670CB00013B/2545